Crosscurrents / Modern Critiques Third Series

Edited by Jerome Klinkowitz

In Form: Digressions on the Act of Fiction
by Ronald Sukenick

Jerome Klinkowitz

LITERARY SUBVERSIONS
New American Fiction and the Practice of Criticism

Southern Illinois University Press
CARBONDALE AND EDWARDSVILLE

Library of Congress Cataloging in Publication Data

Klinkowitz, Jerome.
  Literary subversions.

  (Crosscurrents/modern critiques. Third series)
  Includes bibliographies and index.
    1. American fiction—20th century—History and
criticism.   2. Literature, Experimental—History and
criticism.   3. Criticism—United States—History—20th
century.   I. Title.   II. Series.
PS379.K5525   1985   813′.54′09   85-1887
ISBN 0-8093-1209-3

Printed in the United States of America
Edited by Carol Burns
Designed by Design for Publishing
Jacket design by Quentin Fiore
Production supervised by Kathleen Giencke

88 87 86 85   4 3 2 1

For Rob Wilson and *The North American Review*

I mean by *literature* neither a body nor a series of works, nor even a branch of commerce or of teaching, but the complex graph of the traces of a practice, the practice of writing. Hence, it is essentially the text with which I am concerned— the fabric of signifiers which constitute the work. For the text is the very outcropping of speech, and it is within speech that speech must be fought, led astray—not by the message of which it is the instrument, but by the play of words of which it is the theater. Thus I can say without differentiation: literature, writing, or text. The forces of freedom which are in literature depend not on the writer's civil person, nor on his political commitment—for he is, after all, only a man among others—nor do they even depend on the doctrinal content of his work, but rather on the labor of displacement he brings to bear upon the language. . . . Because it *stages* language instead of simply using it, literature feeds knowledge into the machine of infinite reflexivity. Through writing, knowledge ceaselessly reflects on knowledge, in terms of a discourse which is no longer epistemological, but dramatic. . . . Writing makes knowledge festive.

—Roland Barthes, *Inaugural Lecture*,
Collège de France (1977)

Contents

Crosscurrents/ Modern Critiques/ Third Series

IN THE EARLY 1960s, when the Crosscurrents/Modern Critiques series was developed by Harry T. Moore, the contemporary period was still a controversial one for scholarship. Even today, the elusive sense of the present dares critics to rise above mere impressionism and to approach their subject with the same rigors of discipline expected in more traditional areas of study. As the first two series of Crosscurrents books demonstrated, critiquing contemporary culture often means that the writer must be historian, philosopher, sociologist, and bibliographer as well as literary critic, for in many cases these essential preliminary tasks are yet undone.

To the challenges that faced the initial Crosscurrents project have been added those unique to the past two decades: the disruption of conventional techniques by the great surge in innovative writing in the American 1960s just when social and political conditions were being radically transformed, the new worldwide interest in the Magic Realism of South American novelists, the startling experiments of textual and aural poetry from Europe, the emergence of Third World authors, the rising cause of feminism in life and literature, and, most dramatically, the introduction of Continental theory into the previously staid world of Anglo-American literary scholarship. These transformations demand that many traditional treatments be rethought, and part of the new responsibility for Crosscurrents will be to provide such studies.

Contributions to Crosscurrents/Modern Critiques/Third Series will be distinguished by their fresh approaches to established topics and by their opening up of new territories for discourse. When a single author is studied, we hope to present the first book on his or her work or to explore a previously untreated aspect based on new research. Writers who have been critiqued well elsewhere will be studied in comparison with lesser-known figures, sometimes from other cultures, in an effort to broaden our base of understanding. Critical and theoretical works by leading novelists, poets, and dramatists will have a home in Crosscurrents/Modern Critiques/Third Series, as will sampler-introductions to the best in new Americanist criticism written abroad.

The excitement of contemporary studies is that all of its critical practitioners and most of their subjects are alive and working at the same time. One work influences another, bringing to the field a spirit of competition and cooperation that reaches an intensity rarely found in other disciplines. Above all, this third series of Crosscurrents/Modern Critiques will be collegial—a mutual interest in the present moment that can be shared by writer, subject, and reader alike.

Jerome Klinkowitz

Acknowledgments

The past few years have been a difficult time for literary magazines, and not just because of uncertain finances. As I explain in the following pages, both fiction and criticism have undergone disruptive formal transformations, and editors have been caught in the position of not knowing whom should be written about and how. Therefore, I am grateful to the journals which have let me test out both my critical choices and methods. Much earlier versions of some parts of the essays rewritten for this book appeared in *The North American Review, Partisan Review, The American Book Review, Black American Literature Forum, Critique, College English, Missouri Review, Fiction International,* and *The New Republic.* Abroad, I was welcomed into the pages of *Granta* (King's College, Cambridge), *Revue français d'études américaines* (Université de Paris-IV, Sorbonne Nouvelle), *Delta* (Université Paul Valéry, Montpellier), *Kritikon Litterarum* (Universität zu Köln), *Anglo-American Studies* (Universidad de Salamanca), and *Republika* (Yugoslavia). Though literary magazines have been bold in supporting new work, foundations and grants organizations have not, and the refusal of both governmental and private agencies to risk anything other than reaffirmations of an academic and aesthetic status quo (as reported by Richard Kostelanetz in *The Grants Fix*) is a national scandal. Therefore, I am especially grateful for the support I've received from the University of Northern Iowa, which also funds the publication of *The North American Review.* It is to editor Robley Wilson's credit that the oldest literary journal in America (founded in Boston in 1815) has become one of the most open-minded and venturesome, and it is with deep gratitude that I dedicate this book to Rob and his magazine.

Pretext: Criticism and Fiction in an Age of Subversions

Literary critics are rarely under fire and never tested by the high seas of artistic creation. Instead, as John Updike puts it when titling his own collected essays and reviews, they "hug the shoreline" of accepted practices and ideals. Their potshots are taken from behind the cover of their age's standards, and the long progress of the history of ideas—from the Puritan theocracy of America's settlers through the Enlightenment axioms of the founding fathers and the subsequent dialectics of romanticism, realism, naturalism, and modernism—describes nothing so much as the aesthetic fortifications from which critics have made their sallies against the idiosyncracies of literary creation. William Dean Howells is a much more consistent realist in his criticism than in his fiction, just as Frank Norris found naturalism a more coherent standard in *The Responsibilities of the Novelist* than in his own novels. Ask today's innovative fictionist, Donald Barthelme, about his favorite writers, and he'll name several (Walker Percy, Grace Paley) of a different school entirely. Literary criticism, therefore, is a safe harbor indeed, especially in the Anglo-American tradition where few waves have made it past the breakwater of logical continuity.

When critical standards do come under attack, however, the resulting statements take on millenial proportion. "In or about December, 1910, human character changed"—writing in 1924, with the modern age just established, Virginia Woolf could choose a pivot for the transformative energy ranging from relativity through Verdun to *The Waste Land* and be believed, even though her statement was self-consciously outrageous. Did it really all come down to the postimpressionist show hitting London, as she said? As a flashy metaphor, why not? By 1924, as Bloomsbury flourished and the American 1920's roared, people knew something in the age's standards had changed and the brighter folks wanted to celebrate it. For such a sweeping transformation, one representative shift was as good as another, since to an artist it all meant generally the same thing.

As a forty-year-old Midwestern American writing in 1984, I have the sense that again something big has changed—that with the last two decades behind us we are now as distant from the postimpressionists' 1910 as they were from the academic masters of the early nineteenth century. But how to pin it down? With infantile prattle about Bob Dylan or The Beatles, dynamite dope, and the sexual revolution? Revolutionary feminism? New Politics? The rise and fall of Lyndon Baines Johnson, Long Binh Jail, Maharishi Mahesh Yogi, Jimi Hendrix, and the American Football League? These wide ranging examples from the culture were symptoms of a radical change in day-to-day existence indicative of a vaguely antiauthoritarian discarding of conventions which once had been considered absolutes, but none is useful as a pivot. Try to explicate postmodernism with any one of them and you'll bring down the house with laughter, especially when you're stuck with a historical style more appropriate to the march of ages and a critical rhetoric which is lamely Aristotelian, no matter how innovative your subject may be.

Consider the easy target Ronald Sukenick makes for Gerald Graff when he uses Carlos Castaneda as evidence for the belief that "part of this cultural turnabout is the discovery that all accounts of our experience, all versions of 'reality,' are of the nature of fiction. . . . 'For a sorcerer,' says Don Juan in *Journey to Ixtlan*, 'reality, or the world we all know, is only a description.' "[1] Surrender to someone else's account as being authoritatively true, Sukenick argues, and you open the door to fascism by letting the dictator do your imagining for you. The new fiction, however—like Castaneda's sorcery—undermines such repressive assumptions of order. Sukenick's fiction reflects the same antiauthoritarian impulse which generated much of American 1960s culture—which Graff, as both a social and aesthetic reactionary, can facilely mock. "Licenses to practice epistemological revolution are now as available as handguns," Graff replies, "and any textual leftist can set himself up in business by claiming his peculiar form of linguistic sport threatens the ruling class. But the very facility of such claims makes them suspect."[2]

Therefore, more cautious critics, far from the American Midwest, have removed the essentials of our cultural change to more respectable realms: from the turbulent later 1960s to a decade before, and away from Ron Sukenick's California Pop to that provincially remote intellectual enclave, New York City. As Guy Scarpetta argues from Reims:

In Europe, and in France in particular, we are witnessing today a dubious nostalgia for the American late Sixties and its former, somewhat faded glories. This paper sees in the phenomenon a symptom of the delay and the difficulty with which American modernity is received here; it is also a reminder that genuine 'post-modern' experimental art has its foundations not in the popular ef-florescence of the late Sixties, but in the decisive breakthrough of the late Fifties and early Sixties, in the work which clustered around the Judson Church Dance Theatre, that of Merce Cunningham, Yvonne Rainier, Trisha Brown, Ann Halprin, etc.[3]

Scarpetta is correct in the sense that an avant-garde perceives the movement of a culture years before. But when the kids at Woodstock and after dance for a global audience with a revolutionary sensuosity Yvonne Rainier and Carolee Schneemann still reserve for the experimentalist elite, and when artistically legitimate novels which follow a similarly innovative aesthetic sell in the millions, the case for genuine cultural change is more convincing.

In what way does the "new style" of American 1960s and 1970s fiction reflect "new values"? One need only look at the momentary paralysis of the intellectual avant-garde and the corresponding outburst of activity by its more popularly ac-cessible members to see how an exhausted culture can reform itself and get moving again. On the often quoted first page of his novella, "The Death of the Novel," Sukenick spells out just why conventionally realistic and even modernist fic-tion—narrative grounded in social manners, natural science, psychology, or myth—had run its course, leaving the intellec-tualist writers with little hope beyond silence:

Fiction constitutes a way of looking at the world. Therefore I will begin by considering how the world looks in what I think we may now begin to call the contemporary post-realistic novel. Realistic fiction presupposed chronological time as the medium of a plotted narrative, an irreducible individual psyche as the subject of its characterization, and, above all, the ultimate, concrete reality of things as the object and rationale of its description. In the world

of post-realism, however, all of these absolutes have become absolutely problematic.

The contemporary writer—the writer who is acutely in touch
with the life of which he is a part—is forced to start from scratch:
Reality doesn't exist, time doesn't exist, personality doesn't exist.
God was the omniscient author, but he died; now no one knows the
plot and since our reality lacks the sanction of a creator, there's no
guarantee as to the authenticity of the received version. Time is reduced to presence, the content of a series of discontinuous moments. Time is no longer purposive, and so there is no destiny, only
chance. Reality is, simply, our experience, and objectivity is, of
course, an illusion. Personality, after passing through a phase of
awkward self-consciousness, has become, quite minimally, a mere
locus for our experience. In view of these annihilations, it should be
no surprise that literature, also, does not exist—how could it?
There is only reading and writing, which are things we do, like eating and making love, to pass the time, ways of maintaining a considered boredom in the face of the abyss.

Not to mention a series of overwhelming social dislocations.[4]

Sukenick has described the late modernist world-view which
replaced the cultural beliefs of a previous age—but will he
make the same mistake and ground his fiction in this
"truth," just as earlier writers had supposedly accepted
theirs? Only in the sense that these world-views are fictions
themselves, just another story, as the title of his collection indicates: *The Death of the Novel and Other Stories*. Sukenick's fiction is grounded in itself.

Even as his argument concludes, Sukenick is beginning to
write—and not just in a Beckettian, fill-the-vacuum / I-can't-
go-on-I'll-go-on manner which is itself a form of silence. If
existence has truly slipped out of conventionally artistic reach
(in the Aristotelian sense of imitating an action), then literature will have to be something more than our usual mundane
way of "looking at the world." In uncertain times (as Suken-

ick has described them), fiction may need to perform a more primal act. Perhaps it can create a world with a built-in perspective. If so, it would be in its purest form a creatively epistemological endeavor—as artistic expression has always been in primitive cultures which are constantly in the act of creating their world day by day. Were the American 1960s and 1970s like this? In the sense that impending military, economic, and ecological disaster were daily concerns, these recent years have shared with primitive times the notion that unless we do something, life as a meaningful experience will die. Radical changes in terms of worldly experience have swept away our comfortable understandings of life and left us with an existence sometimes chaotic and most times insipidly unimaginative and dull. But reading and writing as epistemological acts are essential to man because they restore dignity and place him at the center from which all sense of reality issues. And that energized appreciation of experience is what follows in Sukenick's novella. "When, through the imagination, the ego manages to reconcile reality with its own needs," Sukenick explains elsewhere, "the formerly insipid landscape is infused with emotion; and reality, since it now seems intensely relevant to the ego, suddenly seems more real."[5] Such is his hope for writerly fiction.

Sukenick's ideas, of course, square with avant-garde thinking, and his thoughts about the fictionality of all discourse fit the theories of language dominant in our century from Saussure down through Derrida and Kristeva. In these terms, the change in human character would be Derrida's death of the book and the birth of writing. But how is this change popularly expressed, and what new cultural values stand behind it?

Kurt Vonnegut's fiction of the 1960s is the popular artifact which may be the fairest example of American cultural change, equivalent as metaphor to the postimpressionist exhibition Woolf saw in 1910. Shunned as distastefully lowbrow by the Judson Church circle and insufficiently commercial to suit the exploitative tastes of high-power publishers, Vonnegut's fiction limped along for years on the genuinely democratic basis of family magazine and pulp paperback circulation. Then in the late 1960s, as the culture as a whole exploded, Vonnegut was able to write and publish a novel, *Slaughterhouse-Five*, which so perfectly caught America's transformative mood that its story and structure became best-selling metaphors for the new age.

Slaughterhouse-Five is just the type of reinvention which Sukenick admired in Carlos Castaneda's anthropology and urged for postmodern fiction. It ranks as the first widely popular American novel to abandon the traditional structure of linear time and solidly fixable space, even though by virtue of TV-centered temporal existence and increasingly fluid spatial mobility people had been living such innovative lives for a decade at least. In *Slaughterhouse-Five*, there is no discursive message, for its structure and theme are identical: no meaning exists beyond the book's own being. For the sake of a good story, Vonnegut projects one aspect of this new mode as life on the science-fictional planet, Tralfamadore, though he draws an equal number of parallels to the most common elements of middle class life as they've evolved in recent years. The major parallel is *Slaughterhouse-Five* itself, the popular best-seller which fits a Tralfamadorian's description of novels back home:

Each clump of symbols is a brief, urgent message—describing a situation, a scene. We Tralfamadorians read them all at once, not one after the other. There isn't any particular relationship between all the messages, except that the author has chosen them carefully, so that, when seen all at once, they produce an image of life that is beautiful and surprising and deep. There is no beginning, no middle, no end, no suspense, no moral, no causes, no effects. What we love in our books are the depths of many marvelous moments seen all at one time.[6]

Once Vonnegut's protagonist learns this new structural sense, he is anxious to tell his countrymen the good news, for by living out of synch with the culture their lives have become disappointing and frustrating. An optometrist by profession, "he was doing nothing less now, he thought, than prescribing corrective lenses for Earthling souls. So many of those souls were lost and wretched, Billy believed, because they could not see as well as his little green friends on Tralfamadore" (p. 25). And once popular readers learned to handle fiction in an approximation of this manner (*Slaughterhouse-Five* is rigged to discourage any cumulatively serial effect), they spread the word of Vonnegut's appeal and his writer's career was established.

Is the Tralfamadorian view of life (which we might call the 1960s radical perspective) any more reliable than the superannuated beliefs from the 1950s which became so useless in the later turmoil? And is *Slaughterhouse-Five* the only way to write fiction? Not at all, Vonnegut's novel insists, for that is not the point. "Reality" is only a description, as Sukenick indicated in Castaneda's work, as Vonnegut learned studying anthropology, and as the novel's characters keep reminding themselves. One of them explains that "everything there was to know about life was in *The Brothers Karamazov* by Feodor Dostoevsky. 'But that isn't *enough* any more,'" he concludes (p. 87). Readers need new self-created definitions, "wonderful *new* lies, or people just aren't going to want to go on living" (p. 88).

Reminding the reader that fictions are provisional realities and not bedrock truth is the essence of Vonnegut's work, his one enduring theme and the metafictional center to each of his novels. *Cat's Cradle* invents a religion whose very doctrine prevents itself from being taken seriously, and describes the writing of a book which turns out to be the novel in one's hands.[7] On each count, Vonnegut manages to create a fiction without demanding the suspension of disbelief—indeed, the lack of illusion is what both the invented religion and the fabricated book are about. Humans create their own meanings—in religions and in novels, each of which must remain properly *fictional* for the magic to work. Meaning resides not in the content of a novel or in a religion's material beliefs, but rather in the business of setting those things up. The content is not to be taken seriously—otherwise, it becomes the stuff of great mischief as fictional characters are gossiped about like scandalous neighbors and holy wars are waged over what were originally meant to be harmless rituals. Even worse, from an aesthetic point of view, once the materials of novels or religions are taken as the one and only truth, their art evaporates to leave us with content alone, which deteriorates into just that much unformed chaos from our quotidian lives.

Fictional art and not a streamlined version of popular sociology is what the quotidian needs to be rescued from its own banality and temptations toward the authoritarian. To keep in touch with his world yet still maintain his fictionist's posture, Vonnegut has invented a science-fiction novelist named Kilgore Trout who, in the manner of Jorge Luis Borges, provides a canon of unwritten yet eminently quotable works addressed to immediate human needs. Trout appears, reappears, is set free, and is then reinvented (and reenlisted) in four of Vonnegut's five novels published since 1965, and he shows no signs of disappearing from his creator's future work. As a metafictional construct, Trout is free to do in fact what Vonnegut himself does only by implication: to reexamine the facts of life and see how they have changed, then help modify our perception of that provisional reality in order to make it meaningful. Only a false dogmatism can thwart this process, and that is what the new fiction so carefully avoids. Reality is a description—this was the discovery average Americans made in the 1960s as age-old myths of personhood and national character were challenged and in part overturned. That writing as *writing* could be helpful in accommodating these changes was the equally momentous discovery in American fiction.

Once theme becomes structure, fictional meaning finds its place in the process of writing rather than in the static, finished product. Process is kept alive, in an abstractly expressionist manner, by the reader's participation in the novel's act of being. Here is where contemporary culture and popularly accessible literary process coincide with earlier avantgarde breakthroughs, including the Judson Church Dance Theatre but also the nonpredictable music of John Cage and even farther back to the action painting of Hofmann, Pollock, Kline, and de Kooning—an experimentalist tradition reaching back some forty years, stretching beyond New York to Wyoming and the desert Southwest at one extreme and to Europe at the other, all in response to the smug authoritarianism which defined the last stages of modernism in both politics and art.

How does fiction proceed beyond its revolutionary, anti-Aristotelian stage? Is there a productively *non*-Aristotelian or *a*-Aristotelian future for those who follow Sukenick and Vonnegut? Taking the cue once more from language-based studies (while keeping an eye on the culture's attitude toward authoritarian structures in general), the question would be whether the "signs" of conventionally realistic fiction can be used in unconventional ways. What happens, in other words, when these signals are no longer pass-through structures to their referential objects but rather things in themselves? Need fiction exist without all the bits and pieces of life which have filled realistic novels: makes of cars, tastes in music and food, styles and qualities of clothes, all of which the realists use as handy cues to attitudes and themes? "Such signals are dangerous," Gilbert Sorrentino warns, because they "assure us that we are here, oh yes, in the world that we understand"—whereas what we really understand are just the signals themselves.[8] Once that proper understanding is translated into an aesthetic for fiction, the materials of a formerly naive realism may be used for themselves rather than for the presumed reactions they trigger in an unimaginative readership.

Such "experimental realism" differs from the nouveau roman by focusing on the sign as a convention rather than by stripping away societal assumptions from the object itself (as we find Robbe-Grillet & Cie doing). It may be found in the fiction of such diverse talents as Peter Handke, Stephen Dixon, Kenneth Gangemi, Guy Davenport, and Walter Abish—particularly in Abish's *How German Is It*, which builds a fully imagined account of life in the Federal Republic from the surface conventions of social and political life, all of which are provisionally assumed (as they must be in any fluid postwar society).[9] Meanwhile, Vonnegut reimagines American history from the New Deal to Watergate (*Jailbird*),[10] and Sukenick replaces the street signs of poststructuralist Paris with the line-up card of the postwar Brooklyn Dodgers (*Long Talking Bad Conditions Blues*).[11] By discarding realist assumptions, the best of realistic conventions are saved, and both the novel and its surrounding culture live again.

This radical transformation of fiction, however, has led to serious problems in American criticism, for the innovations in literary art ran head-on into a critical tradition by its very essence opposed to even the consideration of nonmimetic devices. The postmodernist disruption of conventional standards was of course a blow to critical orthodoxy everywhere, leading to a notorious squabble between the academic establishment's Raymond Picard and the younger upstart Roland Barthes in France, and to a similar battle in South America over the "boom" called Magic Realism. In the United States, however, there were few intellectual forums in which to carry on the debate. The results were two decades of knee-jerk responses while the new fiction struggled to articulate its own aesthetic, since properly intellectual response has until very recently lagged behind.

The critical and symbolic nature of America itself has traditionally preempted the role of "intellectuals" in American letters. In the eighteenth century, our intellectual spokesmen were practical politicians; in the nineteenth century, they were, more often than not, preachers or editors; and in modern times, they have survived only as working critics—figures such as Edmund Wilson, Malcolm Cowley, and Alfred Kazin, who performed the day-to-day role of critical assessment through literary editorships or even journalism. The intellectual nature of the American experiment, they would say, is evident each day the Constitution and its continuing Amendments operate. As for intellectual thought itself, it remains imbedded in the self-consciously American works of literature: *Moby-Dick, Leaves of Grass, The Great Gatsby*, and the like. As far as the loftier and deeper doubts, our artists have done our thinking for us.

Only in the present age, when for the first time in its history America found itself seriously threatened from within and without (by massive civil discontent, the loss of the first war in its history, and a deteriorating system of world economics and ecology), has the style of intellectual activity truly asserted itself. Several different philosophies now vie with each other for prominence, but at the heart of each may be found an anxiety with present conditions—a convenient parallel to the subversion of age-old aesthetic assumptions by the new fiction. But times have changed. America now has formidable intellectuals because, for the first time, America is in a very bad way.

Innovations in literature are only one index to the transformed culture. Another, and for critics even more unsettling, has been the revolution in literary theory itself—a virtual invasion from the Continent of exotic and sometimes abstruse doctrines of structuralism, semiotics, reception theory, reader response, and deconstruction. This new wave of criticism has collided with a tradition which was itself conservative even in relation to the staid English-language critical manner, thematically oriented and moral in tone, which preceded the French, German, and Swiss eruptions characterized by Jacques Derrida, Wolfgang Iser, and Georges Poulet.

"There are few American writings that require careful analysis and merit intensive study as masterpieces";[12] "American literature is a branch of English literature, as truly as are English books written in Scotland or South Africa."[13] These disclaimers, made by the two scholars who inaugurated the study of their subject at the start of this century, describe an academic conservativism which has crippled the curriculum through the present day. Although the British ideal has faded in favor of the nineteenth-century American and High Modernist classics about which John Macy and William B. Cairns had been so diffident, academic managers of the contemporary remain a cautious and dourly moral lot.

"Crazy is ugly and God don't love ugly": critic and teacher Frank D. McConnell admiringly quotes his fundamentalist student and agrees that the characteristic literary works of our day belong on some index of forbidden books. McConnell urges that these achievements, so notably described in Tony Tanner's *City of Words*, must be replaced by a style more compatible with St. Augustine's "City of God."[14] That present culture may be incapable of such achronistic expression is a signal for moral rearmament; our fundamentalist students must be served.

McConnell's doubts about the present are shared by a large and influential body of teacher-critics, all of whom are reluctant to fall in step with the ranks of contemporary literature. Alfred Kazin, who helped establish Saul Bellow as an intellectually acclaimed (and widely taught) novelist, is just as eager to steer students away from a writer more characteristic of our times, Donald Barthelme. "Is Barthelme a 'novelist'?" Kazin asks, and decides for us: "He is one of the few authentic examples of the 'anti-novelist'—that is, he operates by countermeasures only, and the system that is his own joy to attack permits him what an authoritarian system always permits its lonely dissenters: the sense of their own weakness." Barthelme's themes strike Kazin as fragmented, negativistic, and dull. As for the true action of this writer's story, which takes place within the verbal play of language, "Barthelme sentences us right back again to sentences constructed vindictively of American newspeak."[15] For the language he approves of and calls "style," Kazin chooses a European model—Nabokov—or even better, the language of Joyce, which is safely substructured in myth.

An author without palpable content, such as Barthelme, can have no moral message—and for Kazin messages are what contemporaries need to teach. *God instructs; heroes enact; and poets record*. So reads John Gardner's prescription for literature and its role in the world; teachers must address themselves to all three, becoming theologians and sociologists as well as critics of literary expression.[16] And when the culture changes and literature can turn its tasks to something else, woe to the profligate writers! Pearl K. Bell condemns them as "celebrants of unreason, chaos, and inexorable decay . . . a horde of mini-Jeremiahs crying havoc in the Western world," and Nathan Scott agrees (right down to the same pejorative metaphor) that these writers are being read "by the hordes of those long-haired, jean-clad, pot-smoking bohemians who have entered the world of psychedelia."[17] Aesthetic and intellectual change of recent years is inevitably associated with the more ephemeral qualities of pop culture and dismissed in the same breath. Gerald Graff takes Robert Scholes' more thoughtful explanation of contemporary literature (a willing transcendence of the Cartesian split) and mocks, "As somebody who likes to keep his objects pretty firmly 'out there' and 'other' where I can keep an eye on them, I was mystified by this point, though I gathered that it has something to do with Love and Peace."[18] For Graff, creative writing encodes a meaning just as directly as the bottom line of the budget sheets he deals with as a department chairperson. "I believe that literature . . . does make truth claims," he argues, "and makes them in the same way nonliterary statements do . . . a special kind of truth, no."[19]

These opinions about contemporary American writing have their precedents. It is questionable whether the literary curriculum has ever fairly represented the contemporary. Most of our major writers were untaught in their heyday, waiting until death or fallow periods of decline for resurrection in universities and schools at the hands of a sympathetic professor—witness the academic fortunes of Melville (the hand of Raymond Weaver), Faulkner (Malcolm Cowley), Fitzgerald (Arthur Mizener), Hemingway (Philip Young), and countless more. Other writers, such as T. S. Eliot, are enshrined at the head of a tradition which is then artifically sustained by self-designated professor-poets, while the anti-academic work of Whitman, Williams, Olson, and Frank O'Hara toils on far from the seminars and survey courses. Once established, the academic styles efface what was and is really being read until a whole secondary industry must go back to figure out what else was happening while Melville was being ignored (consider Henry Nash Smith's *Democracy and the Novel: Popular Resistance to Classic American Writers*).

In this respect, the academic tradition has always been conservative. For years, American novel courses ended with Robert Penn Warren's *All the King's Men*, until the Jewish-American tradition grew strong enough to lobby for Bellow or Malamud. Only token examples of books which actually sold in bookstores (and drugstores and airports) were allowed in, and then because of massive extraliterary pressure: from the 1960s counterculture which carried *Catch-22* and *One Flew Over the Cuckoo's Nest* to underground eminence (each sold over fifteen million copies without benefit of a single best-seller list appearance) to the youth market which catapulted Kurt Vonnegut to national fame. Legitimate favorites of the middle class are consigned to their own subcurriculum, popular culture. Meanwhile the academic imprimaturs, as John O'Hara learned, can be struggled for but rarely won. Just a few immortals can be inducted for each age, only so many books taught each semester.

In our own day, academic acceptance seems harder than ever to achieve. While certain token innovationists (actually backward looking in their Aristotelian use of mimetic structures) are favored by those professors whose educations these heavily referential works flatter (classicism for John Barth, modern philosophy and history of science for Thomas Pynchon), the major developments in fiction (and, until very recently, poetry) have been derided as unworthy of instruction. Books which advertise themselves as introductions to current work, such as the *Harvard Guide to Contemporary American Writing*,[20] are almost always limited to the subject matter of literature, in which the artist's role is one of therapist to social reality, the critic's one of pathologist. Such treatment may be partially appropriate in Leo Braudy's chapter on "Realists, Naturalists, and Novelists of Manners" and finds its place even in Lewis P. Simpson's "Southern Fiction" and Mark Schechner's piece on "Jewish Writers." But for "Experimental Fiction," that body of current work which has stood representation on its head, disavowing mimesis in favor of works which linguistically study themselves, how responsible can Josephine Hendin be when she announces the limits of her inquiry: "Postwar experimental fiction may be seen as a search for ways to deal with the violence, brevity, and rigidity of life" (p. 240)? She treats her subject by denying it. "Innovative in neither style nor form," we are told, "postwar experimental fiction uses modernist or standard literary devices to conduct its own experiments with human subjects." How can this describe Donald Barthelme's disjointed narrative, *Snow White*, which refuses to allow its readers to suspend disbelief by tossing in checklists from commercial culture and by stopping everything to quiz the reader on the book so far? Or Richard Brautigan's rupture of narrative itself with a display of self-conscious metaphors which sunder the elements of story in favor of virtuosity on the page? "Experimental man's life is ruled by fragmentation of personality," Hendin replies. "Fragmentation of character and narrative often serve as devices for allaying anxiety" (p. 241). So rather than study their literary art, we had best get the authors themselves on the couch to find out just why they can't write socially helpful books like *All the King's Men*.

To proceed this way diminishes the curriculum. It is hard to imagine the study of contemporary American fiction without a word on Joseph Heller's *Catch-22*, but Hendin ignores it entirely. The vastly inferior *Something Happened* with its anxious and confused protagonist, Bob Slocum, fits her psychoanalytic thesis far better than the surreal syntax of Yossarian's trans-psychological world. What of Chief Broom's metaphoric way of narrative in *One Flew Over the Cuckoo's Nest*? Nothing at all—just a white paper report on the mental ward abuses Ken Kesey has used to get things going. And far better, for Hendin's purpose, to bemoan Billy Pilgrim's "pessimistic and humiliating passivity" (p. 259) than to consider the form of his perception, which shapes Kurt Vonnegut's innovatively spatial novel.

If this is how it is described, in a book intended as a guide for teachers and students, how then can we imagine contemporary fiction is taught? If Hendin is our guide, it would come down to speculation about each author's hangups, with discussion of the books themselves reduced to gossip about real-life images for characters which are, in truth, really words on the page. "One does not make poetry with ideas, but with words," Mallarmé warned, and in our own day William H. Gass has dramatized the case that needs to be studied by teachers who insist that characters are real only when they walk off the page. "It seems a country-headed thing to say," Gass admits, "that literature is language, that stories and the places and the people in them are merely made of words as chairs are made of smoothed sticks and sometimes of cloth or metal tubes. . . . It seems incredible," he sympathizes, "the ease with which we sink through books quite out of sight, pass clamorous pages into soundless dreams." Defining the problem Hendin feels with her allegiance to the social world of human problems, Gass agrees that literature can play tricks. "That novels should be made of words, and merely words, is shocking, really. It's as though you had discovered that your wife were made of rubber; the bliss of all those years, the fears . . . from sponge."[21]

Because of their reluctance to face up to Gass' perception of the verbal character of literature, teachers stay with the cozily human attributes of character and action, like a dog curling up with its master's slipper. Such practice would be of doubtful value for any period of literature, but within the special aesthetic of contemporary innovative fiction it is contradictory, for such illusionary features are just what authors have disclaimed for their works. "Novels are cluttered with all kinds of signals," Gilbert Sorrentino explains, "flashing and gesturing so that the author may direct our attention to a particular configuration of character or plot in order that his work, such as it is, may be made simpler for him, and for us." But in fact we are only "being told what we already know."[22] These, of course, are just the materials Hendin chooses to write about and to teach. Sorrentino condemns them as the death of literary art, for "they allow the writer to slip out from under the problems that only confrontation with his materials can solve" (p. 196).

What is the substance of that confrontation? Words. "The novel must exist outside of the life it deals with; it is not an imitation," Sorrentino argues, reminding us that for all their referential quality, words are still things in themselves, subject to artistic ordering. "The novel is an invention, something that is made; it is not an expression of 'self'; it does not mirror reality. If it is any good at all it mirrors the processes of the real. . . . We find, not the meaning of life, but a revelation of its actuality" like that given by the more plastic arts (pp. 196-97). True novelists, Donald Barthelme adds, "modify the world by adding to its store of objects the literary object—which is then encountered in the same way as other objects in the world." Here is true content: "The reader is not listening to an authoritative account of the world delivered by an expert (Faulkner on Mississippi, Hemingway on the corrida) but bumping into something that is *there*, like a rock or a refrigerator."[23] As Ronald Sukenick puts it, the world is already full of news and news sources; fiction is our response to the news, a humanly expressive action and not the shabbily secondhand imitation of something more real than itself.[24]

Critics and teachers a generation younger than those writing for the *Harvard Guide* have found the current period to be one of bold innovation indeed. The heroic models and ideals which the moralist professors prefer "have been made outmoded by changes in the nature of the modern world and in the nature of man's relation to it," argues Larry McCaffery. A universe which is now seen as "indeterminate, uncertain, chaotic, or relative" simply will not support the "optimistic or humanistic premises" which underlie traditionalist art and ways of teaching it.[25] Instead, literature has kept pace with science and philosophy, to the point of agreeing that all fictions are primarily systems of meaning which owe the standards of their success to internal consistency and not to the way in which they mimetically represent the outside world. Yet so often when contemporary novels are taught, the final judgments reflect and sustain conventional opinions in the outside world about what is real, and how it is ordered, and what matters in it. Why do we hear so much of Joyce Carol Oates, John Updike, or Walker Percy? Because the nature of their work, written according to a nineteenth-century notion of mimesis, "ends up interpreting the present by reference to a preestablished code of values inherited from bygone days." Hence, Mas'ud Zavarzadeh suggests that "their fiction, consequently, turns out to be either the fiction of entertainment or, in the most dangerous sense of the word, escapist fiction. They ignore the newness of new realities and, by inventing a myth of continuity based on an assumption of a coherent external reality, lie to their readers as they give false assurances about a nonexistent order."[26]

Consider how Paramount Films condenses Ernest Hemingway's *Islands in the Stream* into thirty-six minutes of externally represented action which, according to its educational catalogue, focuses on its author's "most important themes," including "the redeeming qualities of love and commitment" (what one then tells students about the structures of *The Sun Also Rises* and *A Farewell to Arms* is another problem). How is a student to respond to John Updike's story, "The Music School"? First, watch it on educational television, then "explain why you do or don't like Albert Schweigen," the work's protagonist, "by comparing him with the other characters in the story." These fictions, in Zavarzadeh's view, and especially these ways of teaching them, "provide the readers with an escape from the incongruous realities of the times rather than exposing them to an imaginative exploration of such realities" (p. 224).

Contemporary literature is not about experience, it is more experience. Only by closing with this experiential energy—on the level of text—may these works of art be realized for students. The only comparable recent development to be so vehemently resisted by the academic establishment was Abstract Expressionist art. Not until teachers learned that artists such as Jackson Pollock, Willem de Kooning, and Franz Kline regarded the canvas not as a surface on which to represent but rather as an arena in which to act, with paint as its own subject (the scheme is Harold Rosenberg's), did students and their teachers have a framework for understanding just what was happening in the works they were viewing.

Such artwork, of course, believes in its own reality and believes that its integrity can survive the destruction by modern science and philosophy of linear chronology, the irreducible center of character, and the concrete reality of things. Obviously, a compositional sense is as applicable to fiction, poetry, and drama as it is to painting, once the aspect of making takes precedence over representing. "In a generative theory," writes Ronald Sukenick in his "Digressions" essay, "narrative would be the movement of the mind as it organizes the open field of the text. In a vitalistic sense, it would be the energy of personality, reversing the entropy of experience—also known as the 'subject matter,' or 'content,' as it enters the field of the text. The result is new experience, distinguished by the way it salvages energy from that constant dissipation characteristic of the flux" (*NLH,* p. 436; *In Form,* p. 13).

Critiquing literature as human process transcends an easy humanism of subject. Only a moral allegiance to the notion of a world which is under rational, willful control can explain the prejudice which keeps contemporary literature from being taught as it truly is. The question remains for critics to decide if they should be promoting contemporary literature which whispers fairy tales that the world is not mysterious, that it is open to manipulation by writers who would impose a moral ideal derived from something other than expressive art, or whether a more suitable and worthwhile goal might be to study how contemporary writers are working out, in the very practice of their art, the essentials of our fate.

America does now have a full-fledged class of literary intellectuals, sufficiently notorious to be flattered with references even in a popular novel such as John Barth's *Sabbatical* (1982) which enumerates the "literary-critical structuralists, deconstructionists, semioticists, and neo-Nietzscheans of Paris, New Haven, and Milwaukee."[27] Part of this effect is thanks to transplanting, with Jacques Derrida sharing a regular visiting appointment at Yale and Julia Kristeva enjoying similar status at Columbia. But the Yale group has its Geoffrey Hartman, J. Hillis Miller, Paul de Man, and Harold Bloom, and the University of Wisconsin-Milwaukee has given its prestigious Vilas Professorship to Ihab Hassan. Yet these critics have virtually deserted applied criticism for the more rarified airs of intellectual theory itself, more philosophy than criticism. Ihab Hassan's *Radical Innocence* (1961) has no sequel; instead, its author has gone on to esoterically paracritical investigations of pure mind, an important endeavor but a loss for more immediate problems of contemporary literature. Nor has Robert Scholes' *The Fabulators* (1967), which gave first serious attention to Vonnegut, Barth, Hawkes, and others, led to any further updates beyond a subgeneric interest in science fiction. The criticism of contemporary fiction has been left to partisan sniping over its larger formal and moral issues, while the specific works themselves are critically unread.

Literary Subversions provides individual readings of the novels and story collections central to formal developments of the past few years; but it also furnishes models for various critical approaches aesthetically appropriate to the new styles of literary art. The works chosen for study are representative of the range of standards in play today, from John Barth's lingering Aristotelianism to Ishmael Reed's emphatically multicultural pluralism, and from John Irving's self-generating fictional world to Thomas McGuane's radicalization of the novel of manners. Although not a semiotic or deconstructionist work, *Literary Subversions* is written with an awareness

of the great shift in theory which has confronted the traditional Anglo-American humanistic and even moralistic focus
on thematic content with the revelation—a linguistically air-
tight one!—that the words by which we signify reality are
most apparently signs in themselves, a set of differences with
no real meaning other than their own systematics. That one
can still be a sensitive and insightful reader of texts while employing this vision was proven by the career of Roland
Barthes, and the capstone to his career—the Inaugural Lecture he delivered from the first Chair of Semiotics at the Collège de France in 1977—provides an introduction to this volume's method.

The book itself is formed by four sections: the essay as polemic, as lyric, as meditation, and as witness. Each testifies to
the unique business at hand: arguing a point of aesthetics,
celebrating a triumph of literary form, pondering a work itself dominated by certain issues of thought or affection, and
finally employing the critic's own experience as part of the
critical act. To write a book covering the contemporary scene
in just one of these manners would be to force a thesis, necessarily slighting the idiosyncracies of the works chosen for
comment. Adapting one's critical form to the peculiarities of
the text itself, however, allows those texts to speak through
one's own words—a principal aim of *Literary Subversions*.

"The text is the very outcropping of speech," Barthes reminds us, "and it is within speech that speech must be
fought, led astray—not by the message of which it is the instrument, but by the play of words of which it is the theater."[28] Here is the territory of the essay as polemic, respond-
ing to the central literary battle of our age between mimesis
and artistic self-apparency. John Barth's fiction stands at the
center of this battle, only most recently in *Sabbatical* (1982)
undergoing the transformation between these two poles. The
debate over sources from which words derive their meaning

is escalated into cultural terms by Ishmael Reed, who opposes Barth's Aristotelian and classically European standards with a new multicultural base unique to the Americas. Michel Foucault has demonstrated that cultural norms are established by systems of constraint, and among contemporary Americans Ishmael Reed is the writer most sensitive to this problem. In John Irving's fiction, self-apparency—fictive techniques signalling their own reality rather than a reflection of the outside world—is given full play, with the result that something new is added to the world rather than reproduced from it, transcending the restraints Reed decries. For this entire battle of the books, the polemical essay is appropriate, since it fastens upon the principles of debate and pushes them to their argumentative extreme. It is appropriate to the study of fiction only when that fiction itself builds its effect upon contention, as the readings of *Sabbatical*, Reed's *The Terrible Twos*, and Irving's *The Water-Method Man* show.

There are, however, writers at peace with their material, for whom the critical polemic would be vastly inappropriate. Here the critical lyric takes over as a celebration of masterful technique: John Updike's fusion of transparent mimesis and purely sonorous language in his evocation of growing up, marrying, and divorcing in America; Grace Paley's aesthetic sociology of improvised life in New York; and Robley Wilson's self-conscious delight in the conventions of literary realism. These authors write at a blithesome remove from the polemical struggles described in part one; yet they are an important part of contemporary literature and deserve their own style of commentary. Hence, the lyric contemplation of their work. "The forces of freedom which are in literature," Barthes notes, depend mostly upon "the labor of displacement [the writer] brings to bear upon language" (p. 462), and Updike's grace with words and sentiment, Paley's with language and scene, and Wilson's with the very conventions of narrative themselves all bespeak a craftsmanship which it is criticism's best role to admire.

Lyric contemplations, however, are not appropriate to works in which concern with one topic or technique completely dominates the writer's effect. "Because it *stages* language instead of simply using it," Barthes observes, "literature feeds knowledge into the machine of infinite reflexivity . . . in terms of a discourse which is no longer epistemological, but dramatic" (pp. 463–64). In some cases, the resulting work of fiction can be flawed by this emphasis, as is John Gardner's *Grendel* by the author's forced sense of experimentalism. Other times, the effect is quite positive, as with Thomas McGuane's rich meditation on the manners of countercultural America and Richard Yates' obsession with the circumstances of sadness, a theme for which he specially fashions his narrative techniques. Here, a third style of critical approach is needed: a contemplation upon the specific issue apart from the polemics which may have prompted it (the business of writers who present a higher profile in these aesthetic battles, as treated in section one) and independent of a study of craft itself (which is more properly detailed in considering the writers of section two, whose consistency of manner makes such investigations more even and hence more analytically reliable).

Stages one, two, and three are of course preliminary to each other: a specific technical or thematic obsession makes no sense without an understanding of the standards of craftsmanship in a literary age, and those very standards are granted free exercise only by the aesthetic debates which establish them. Obviously, three different types of writing are being practiced in any single age, and criticism must be adaptable to all of them. In terms of an overall theoretical approach, composing a thesis-based literary history of a period would force the critic to adopt something like an Hegelian dialectic or perhaps a model somewhat like Thomas Kuhn's structure of scientific revolutions, tracing the progress of a formal ideal through its various stages of the naive, the critical, and the sophisticated; the former approach had its influence on my own *Literary Disruptions: The Making of a Post-Contemporary American Fiction* (1975), while James Mellard took Kuhn's explicit model for his *The Exploded Form: The Modernist Novel in America* (1980). But such grandly synthesizing methods are worthwhile only for overviews. When it comes to the practical, applied criticism of specific works, it is imperative to adjust one's critical methods to the specific purpose of the literary work at hand, or else the criticism of contemporary literature will turn into a hobby-horse derby of benefit to none.

This adaptability of method is even more crucial when a literary age is in flux, as ours certainly is. Given the self-consciously battle-of-the-books quality of both the creative and critical sides of writing, one is faced with an aesthetic variant of Werner Heisenberg's Uncertainty Principle, which taught that any scientific measurement is compromised by the effective presence of the observer. For the commentator who deals with literature being written in his own times and in some cases before his or her very eyes, the question of one's own presence in the affair becomes central to the critical act. Therefore, section four, the essay as witness, becomes the most important and logically the most idiosyncratic part of *Literary Subversions*, incorporating elements of all three previous methods plus framing the approach through one's own experience with the writing. In our own times, a novel form of response known as The New Journalism has been devised to meet similar problems with the real world of events: dismayed by the confusion inherent in their subject, writers such as Tom Wolfe, Dan Wakefield, and Hunter S. Thompson have found that the most reliable way to handle their reporting assignments is to immerse themselves in the experience and describe what happens to them. In circumstances which defy conventional description—Ken Kesey's busload of merry pranksters, the on- and off-set conspiracies of a TV soap opera, the twisted reality of the drug culture—Wolfe, Wakefield, and Thompson have found that the one thing they can truly report on is themselves, and each has become a master at it. For The New Journalism, each book becomes its own form, since the reporter's experience is never the same. Hence, in the essay as witness, form becomes a new discovery each time around, from the *samizdat* approach to Jerzy Kosinski's oddly unfolding biography to a stack of postcards from novelist Tom Glynn. Having Kosinski spin out a string of cock-and-bull stories and Glynn camp out in your backyard *en famille* can enhance the understanding of their writing but only if the critical form allows itself to be unique to each experience. These essays are certainly one-shots: Kosinski has vowed to tell no more apocryphal stories, and Glynn's postcards will never again be so innocently candid. But neither should the form be repeated for another writer in another set of circumstances in another time. Form is the line of footprints we leave behind us in the sand—such is the richness of literature which criticism must emulate to be equal to its responsive task.

Roland Barthes' concluding dictum, therefore, is appropriate to both the essay as witness and in its overall obligation of response: "Writing makes knowledge festive" (p. 464), a requirement which is no less the critic's duty than the novelist's.

Notes

1. Gerald Graff, *Literature Against Itself* (Chicago: University of Chicago Press, 1979), pp. 171–72, quoting Ronald Sukenick, "Upward and Juanward: The Possible Dream," *Village Voice*, 25 January 1973, pp. 27–28, 30–31; Sukenick's essay is collected in his *In Form: Digressions on the Act of Fiction* (Carbondale: Southern Illinois University Press, 1985), pp. 214–25.
2. Gerald Graff, reply to Ronald Sukenick, *American Book Review* 3 (May–June 1981): 2; Sukenick had reviewed Graff's *Literature Against Itself* in the previous issue: *American Book Review* 3 (March–April 1981): 5.
3. Editor's abstract to Guy Scarpetta, "Quelques notes sur la 'post modernité,'" *Revue française d'études américaines*, No. 8 (1979), pp. 203–13.
4. Ronald Sukenick, "The Death of the Novel," in *The Death of the Novel and Other Stories* (New York: Dial Press, 1969), p. 41.
5. Ronald Sukenick, *Wallace Stevens: Musing the Obscure* (New York: New York University Press, 1967), pp. 14–15. Collected in Sukenick's *In Form*, p. 174.
6. Kurt Vonnegut, Jr., *Slaughterhouse-Five* (New York: Delacorte Press/Seymour Lawrence, 1969), p. 76.
7. Kurt Vonnegut, Jr., *Cat's Cradle* (New York: Holt, Rinehart, & Winston, 1963). This novel was contracted as a paperback original in 1961, but was issued in hardcover under a contract option in 1963 to few reviews and small sales, and did not begin to reach a wide readership until its new paperback edition in 1970 (on the heels of Vonnegut's sudden fame).
8. Gilbert Sorrentino, "The Various Isolated: W. C. Williams' Prose," *New American Review*, No. 15 (1972), p. 195.
9. Walter Abish, *How German Is It* (New York: New Directions, 1980). For a full analysis, see Jerome Klinkowitz, "Walter Abish and the Surfaces of Life," *Georgia Review* 35 (1981): 416–20; for an interesting response from the Federal Republic, see "Literatur: Nun Liebchen," *Der Spiegel* 8 June 1981, pp. 195–97.
10. Kurt Vonnegut, *Jailbird* (New York: Delacorte Press/Seymour Lawrence, 1979).

11. Ronald Sukenick, *Long Talking Bad Conditions Blues* (New York: Fiction Collective, 1979).

12. William B. Cairns, *A History of American Literature* (New York: Oxford University Press, 1912), p. v.

13. John Macy, *The Spirit of American Literature* (New York: Dodd, Mead and Co., 1911), p. 3.

14. *Four Postwar American Novelists* (Chicago: University of Chicago Press, 1977), p. xvi.

15. *Bright Book of Life* (Boston: Atlantic/Little, Brown, 1973), p. 273.

16. *On Moral Fiction* (New York: Basic Books, 1978), p. 28.

17. Pearl K. Bell, "American Fiction: Forgetting Ordinary Truths," *Dissent* 20 (1973): 26; Nathan A. Scott, Jr., " 'New Heav'ns, New Earth'—the Landscape of Contemporary Apocalypse," *Journal of Religion* 53 (1973): 12–13.

18. Review of Scholes' *Fabulation and Metafiction*, *American Literature* 52 (1980): 134.

19. "Responses and Discussion," *Bulletin of the Midwest Modern Language Association* 13 (1980): 11.

20. Daniel Hoffman, ed. (Cambridge: Harvard University Press, 1979).

21. "The Medium of Fiction," *Fiction and the Figures of Life* (New York: Alfred A. Knopf, 1970), p. 27.

22. "The Various Isolated," p. 195.

23. "After Joyce," *Location*, No. 2 (Summer 1964), p. 13.

24. "Twelve Disgressions Toward a Study of Composition," *New Literary History* 6 (1974–75): 429–37. Collected in Sukenick's *In Form*, pp. 3–15. These sentiments are amplified in the conclusion to *In Form*, pp. 241–43.

25. "The Gass-Gardner Debate: Showdown on Main Street," *The Literary Review* 23 (1979): 139.

26. *The Mythopoeic Reality* (Urbana: University of Illinois Press, 1976), p. 223.

27. John Barth, *Sabbatical* (New York: Putnam, 1982), p. 231.

28. "Inaugural Lecture, Collège de France," trans. Richard Howard, in *A Barthes Reader*, ed. Susan Sontag (New York: Hill & Wang, 1982), p. 462. Originally published as *Leçon* (Paris: Editions du Seuil, 1978).

I. The Essay as Polemic

For the text is the very outcropping of speech, and it is within speech that speech must be fought, led astray—not by the message of which it is the instrument, but by the play of words of which it is the theater.

—R. B.

John Barth: Fiction in an Age of Criticism

IF AMERICAN CRITICS were to follow the practice of their Spanish and Latin American colleagues, John Barth and certain of his contemporaries would be called "the Generation of '31"—a helpful term which has thus far escaped us. Give or take a few years on either side of that date, one can list the birthdates of a whole constellation of fiction writers who for the lack of a better word have been consistently called "young" and "new," even as still newer and fresher ways of writing fiction have come along: John Barth (1930), Donald Barthelme (1931), Ronald Sukenick and Robert Coover (1932), and Jerzy Kosinski (1933), to name only the most commercially prominent. Just a few years older are Raymond Federman, John Hawkes, and William H. Gass; and even fewer years younger are Thomas Pynchon, Clarence Major, Imamu Amiri Baraka, Steve Katz, and Ishmael Reed.

Though their differences are more numerous than their similarities, all have taken part in the trend which, for a time in the late 1960s and early 1970s, brought a new emphasis on antirealism to mainstream American fiction. Often against their will, they have been grouped together as a school of Metafiction, Superfiction, Surfiction, Disruptive Fiction, and the like. Joe David Bellamy's *The New Fiction: Interviews with Innovative American Writers* (Urbana: University of Illinois Press, 1974) and Jack Hicks's anthology, *Cutting Edges: Young American Fiction for the '70s* (New York: Holt, Rinehart & Winston, 1973) are symptomatic of the critical habit of calling these writers collectively "new" and "innovative," tacitly assuming that "youth" (however inappropriate to a writer forty-four years old at the time, or even fifty-one) is superior to "age" and that "innovative" means "better," in the sense of a new and improved product. But virtually no critic or literary historian of these years can evade responsibility for such overly enthusiastic label making. If indeed there was any sort of breakthrough in fiction, never—as many of these same critics now admit—was it so sloppily described.

Quite unhappily at the center of this critical mess stands John Barth, the American fictionist probably most responsible for the boom antirealistic fiction enjoyed for a time among the large commercial publishers. What does Barth truly have in common with his collectively unwilling colleagues, besides sharing their desire to be treated individually and not as part of some critically regimented group? For one thing, and most importantly, he is a member in good standing of American academe. Even before publishing his first novel in 1956, he had earned a graduate degree from Johns Hopkins University and was teaching as a member of Pennsylvania State University's Department of English. Subsequent novels and growing critical fame, enhanced by his reputation as a brilliant teacher, have propelled him from increasingly distinguished professorships at the State University of New York at Buffalo and Boston University to his present post as Alumni Centennial Professor of English and Creative Writing at his alma mater, Johns Hopkins. Virtually every other member of our improvised Generation of '31 is graduate-school trained or oriented and boasts a long (if not continual) association with universities. Most, like Barth, have published significant critical work. In previous literary epochs, American fiction writers have been preachers, plumbers, able-bodied seamen, or workaday journalists, but rarely conventional academics. If for Herman Melville a whaling ship was his Harvard and his Yale, Yale and Harvard (and their sister institutions) have been the whaling ships of a great many writers of the Generation of '31.

Other correspondences are just as easy to note. Women are conspicuously absent, though the popularity of Anaïs Nin which crowned her later years and the example of Englishwoman Doris Lessing have inspired critical attention for anti-realistic work by American women writers in more recent years. And although few of the Generation of '31 have been consistently anti-realistic throughout their careers, the prominence of their self-reflective fictions in the minds of critical adversaries has led to a violent backlash against the style. This reaction was articulated most comprehensively for fiction in John Gardner's *On Moral Fiction* (New York: Basic Books, 1978) and for critical theory in Gerald Graff's *Literature Against Itself* (Chicago: University of Chicago Press, 1979). Succeeding generations of writers, particularly the M.F.A. graduates of programs such as the University of Iowa's Writers' Workshop, have tended on the whole to turn away from self-conscious innovation as sternly as the Pop Art and Hard Edge painters of the 1960s rejected the "action painting" of the Abstract Expressionists dominant in the 1940s and 1950s—simply as a gesture of creative independence, perhaps for fresher fields of economic gain, and most certainly because the ground floor opened by the higher education boom had been filled up and closed.

What becomes clear in terms of simple historical observation (something much easier from the distance of 1984) is that the self-reflective innovationists of the Generation of '31 wrote their fiction under tremendous critical pressure: having been told that because of realism's eclipse the novel was dead, they felt compelled to challenge and hopefully reinvent conventions of fiction which in terms of the mainstream had been fairly stable since the days of Fitzgerald, Hemingway, and Faulkner. But the very success of their work—artistically, commercially, and philosophically—served many contrary interests. Like the "Boom in Spanish American Literature" described with no small irony by one of its participants, José Donoso, in his book of that name (New York: Columbia University Press, 1977; first published in Spanish as *Historia personal del "boom"* by Editorial Anagrama, Barcelona, 1972), America's momentary boom in anti-realistic fiction has been more useful as a descriptive tool for its enemies. For its writers, the effects have been at times debilitating. Writing novels in an age of criticism, when the very life of fiction is a matter of hot and often vicious debate, has been no easy pleasure.

"*In a sense, I am Jacob Horner,*" proclaims the narrator of John Barth's second novel, *The End of the Road* (New York: Appleton-Century-Crofts, 1958). Sentenced to a self-consciously absurdist therapy of teaching college English, Barth's narrator reminds us of the dispensation under which Barth himself felt he must write. It was 1958, not 1851; Melville's "Call me Ishmael" was part and parcel of another time, just as Kurt Vonnegut's invocational "Call me Jonah" for *Cat's Cradle* (1963) would entertain the same heartbreaking paradox of having to (yet being unable to) write a Great American Novel for our times—an era which, as Barth saw it, had rejected the Cartesian definition of ego so central to traditional novelistic design. A hero could no longer speak with confidence and coherence and so define himself since under contemporary philosophical pressure the old "cogito, ergo sum" had become a farcically painful lie.

The End of the Road and Barth's first novel, *The Floating Opera* (New York: Appleton-Century-Crofts, 1956), were written in the same burst of creative energy during the mid-1950s, when the promise of commercial publication drove Barth to a frenzy of literary production he has not since matched (as noted by David Morrell in *John Barth: An Introduction* [University Park: Pennsylvania State University Press, 1976]). That first work was not to have been a novel at all—"a philosophical minstrel show" is how Barth described his plans, not wanting to write a novel yet hoping to make it "a work of literature" nevertheless (p. 12). In form, both books turned out to be rather conventional novels in the then-popular style of André Malraux, Albert Camus, and other such thinkers. Each was heavily philosophical, and the first brushed so close with absolute nihilism that its original publishers insisted on a different, more humanistically acceptable ending. (Barth's preferred text is found in the revised and restored edition published by Doubleday in 1967.) But these initial works won Barth the beginnings of a substantial following: not among the reading public (for Morrell estimates less than 5,000 copies of the two books were sold), but with John Barth's colleagues in the profession of English. A knowledge of literary and philosophical tradition complemented by the life-experience of teaching these verities were the qualifications of Barth's ideal reader.

"My Uncle Mike, the Zen Philosopher, says it wouldn't make any difference to him if he was *dead or alive*!" reads a popular children's cartoon of the 1960s, showing two little kids sitting in a treehouse with their scuffed sneakers and baseball cards, tossing this Zen wisdom back and forth. "Well, if he feels *that* way," one kid argues, "why don't he *kill* his self?" The other kid's answer is the same as John Barth's: "He says 'cause it *wouldn't make any difference*!" This attitude, so easily satirized in the Sunday comics, was more somber stuff in the 1950s when Barth wrote *The Floating Opera* and *The End of the Road*. Todd Andrews of the first novel lives with a heart which any moment might stop ticking, or so his doctor tells him; Jake Horner of the second book teaches English as medically prescribed therapy for his crisis of identity. Barth fleshes out their intellectual problems with—to a man of his generation and profession—the most salaciously flirtatious of actions: the invitation from a consenting husband to bed the latter's wife, in both cases a seeming triumph of the cultured mind over the messy limits of emotions. To some extent life has bored each protagonist, but neither is willing to risk it. Others take that risk for them: in the second novel a woman dies, and a whole boatload of persons in the first are saved only by the most whimsical chance. Emotional casualties litter each novel, but the narrator-protagonists survive to walk full circle back to their novels' beginnings, themselves unchanged by the entire catastrophic experience. All that's been confirmed are their own initial suspicions (about time in the first book, about identity in the second), which started things rolling in the first place. The most sterling survivor is tradition, for in both novels it has been left perfectly intact.

John Barth's work in fiction has been to one end: the employment of literary exhaustion as a device against itself. Barth's eloquent justification of this technique was published as "The Literature of Exhaustion" in *The Atlantic* (August 1967); but nearly a year before, in *Commentary* (October 1966), critic Robert Garis had perceived just what Barth was doing. *The Floating Opera*, Garis noted, was "modeled on *Tristram Shandy* (amusing inability to get down to telling the story)," while *The End of the Road*, he might have added, was an almost perfect rehearsal of forms and themes prominent in postwar European existentialism. (In fact, Garis argued that the Jake Horner novel was an excellent dramatization of Barth's academic times.) Garis did proceed to check off Barth's next two novels as further self-apparent literary exercises—*The Sot-Weed Factor* (New York: Doubleday, 1960) being "an 806-page literal imitation of every picaresque novel from Rabelais to *Fanny Hill*" and *Giles Goat-Boy* (New York: Doubleday, 1966) as "a 710-page pseudo-adaptation of the Swift of *Gulliver's Travels* and the narrative sections of *A Tale of a Tub*." But unlike Barth's other academic endorsers, Garis was strongly critical of this tactic. "I call what Barth is doing Baconianism," he complained,

because, as the length itself of the two latter books might suggest, one sees here a heartbreakingly obsessive patience and persistence; and yet, it doesn't work. Just as the Baconians in the end tell us nothing about Shakespeare, so Barth's laborious imitations fail to produce interesting or important works of art. An extremely talented novelist has, for motives one can only guess at, deliberately turned himself into a kind of mad graduate student in English literature.

John Barth's motives were clarified in his "Literature of Exhaustion" essay published in *The Atlantic* ten months later, and a sequel called "The Literature of Replenishment" for the same magazine's January 1980 issue added further commentary pertinent to his booklength works of the intervening years: *Lost in the Funhouse: Fiction for Print, Tape, Live Voice* (New York: Doubleday, 1967), *Chimera* (New York: Random House, 1972), and *Letters: A Novel* (New York: Putnam's, 1979). Why should a contemporary American novelist use the form of Henry Fielding in 1960? Or of Samuel Richardson in 1979? Should the literary aspirations of our age be "*Tom Jones* by Samuel Beckett? Saarinen's Parthenon, D. H. Lawrence's *Wuthering Heights, The 1001 Nights* by John Barth?" as the first essay's subhead playfully asked? Barth the critic went on to explain that any educated writer in this day and age was faced with "the used-upness of certain forms or exhaustion of certain possibilities—by no means necessarily a cause for despair." In his 1980 sequel, Barth adds that any writer, in any age, faces such exhaustion, as disclaimers from the earliest Egyptian scribes suggest. The literary work of John Barth, however, employs these ultimacies against themselves. In the years since Barth published his first essay, a panoply of theories to explain such authorial practice have flooded America, from the "anxiety of influence" operative upon writers to the "reception theory" which might describe the role of any natural reader. But if we are to trust the teller before the tale (something most traditional critics tell us not to do), we must take Barth's word that he has been writing this way to counteract the tendencies he sees in other contemporary art, which he insists falls short of genuine aesthetic achievement.

The Sot-Weed Factor and *Giles Goat-Boy* employ various eighteenth-century conventions to make their own twentieth-century artistic statements. In the former, the secret journal of a character named Henry Burlingame is framed within the narrative adventures of the poet, Ebenezer Cooke; and all of the familiar Fieldingesque techniques, so tedious themselves in the hands of anyone else but their inventor, are interesting and entertaining because they must be read not as the product of a third-rate contemporary but instead as the studied parody by a brilliant scholar of Fielding's art. In similar manner, *Giles Goat-Boy* takes what it can from Swift, substituting an allegory of mid-twentieth-century academic politics as a comment on the state of the world ("University" for "Universe," "Twelve-Term Riot" for "World War II," and so forth). As technique, the transpositions from Fielding and Swift are flawless; but as Robert Garis and others have complained, they are only technique, offering no new perspective at all and telling readers nothing they do not already know. *Lost in the Funhouse* and *Chimera* are more deliberate investigations of narrative itself, including a cut-out Moebius strip, a series of quoted quotes successively swallowed up by the necessary punctuation marks, a story which narrates its own inception and dissolution, and various retellings of ancient myths. *Letters* functions as a coda to Barth's entire literary career so far, for its seven epistolary authors who exchange correspondence among themselves are either characters from the previous six books or are John Barth himself and his fresh creations.

This seven-book canon, no small achievement for a writer born in 1931, would be the perfect index of a literary age except for one fact, which its author keeps repeating in his influential essays: he does not sympathize with the spirit of his times. "The Literature of Exhaustion" opens with a playfully sarcastic dismissal of a style of work then being produced by a young writer-publisher outside the conservative academic community: Dick Higgins and his Something Else Press (Higgins's own essay, "Intermedia" [1966], is reprinted in Higgin's *foew&ombwhnw* [New York: Something Else Press, 1969] and in his *Horizons: The Poetics and Theory of the Intermedia* [Carbondale: Southern Illinois University Press, 1984]). Within this style, Barth included a good sample (but not all properly attributed to their best practitioners) of literary, theatrical, musical, and artistic work unlike his and his academic colleagues' own, including the assemblage novels of Robert Filliou, the Happenings of Allan Kaprow, the nonpredictable music of John Cage, and the Pop Art of Robert Rauschenberg. All were whimsically degraded as lacking seriousness, discipline of effort, and achievement of stable form, as if these were the prime requisites of artistic success—which Barth indeed believed they were. "The New York Correspondence School of Literature," as he called them, were capable of interesting ideas for beer-drinking conversation. But they were fully incapable of producing great art.

What Barth overlooked, and what he overlooked more deliberately in his sequel essay of 1980, was nothing less than the history of twentieth-century art. That history, according to even the most conservative of critics, has been the steady effacement of represented action from works of art in all disciplines—whether literary, dramatic, musical, or graphic. Disfavor for such history may be a valid excuse for any person granted an advanced degree before the late 1960s and continuing to teach in the same discipline, since most American graduate schools until then insisted that the subjects of scholarly inquiry be deceased, all pertinent texts established, and all letters and memoirs published or at least open to study. For academic scholarship, such a rule may have merits. But it is hardly an excuse for anyone professing to be on the leading edge of creative achievement.

The aesthetic of mid-century America is traced most easily by the work of artists Barth dismisses as impertinent to his own High Art. The Abstract Expressionist painters active in New York during the 1940s and 1950s (de Kooning, Pollock, and Kline, for example) established, in critic Harold Rosenberg's words, that for this time and place the canvas of one's work (in any medium) was to be less "a surface on which to represent" than "an arena in which to act." The work's own action, and not a representation of an action, would be art's subject. The predictable reaction to this aesthetic by succeeding generations of creative artists did not negate Rosenberg's truth; Pop Art, Hard Edge, Minimal, and Conceptual Art (all products of the years when John Barth has written fiction) simply established new ways of non-Aristotelian expression which could not be merchandised either as imitations of a now-saleable style or as portable objects in themselves. Foremost was the integrity of the unaligned artist, even though those strategies of nonalignment could later be described as movements of their own; "anti-movement" art was the period's capstone. During all these years, however, John Barth was solidly aligned with a tenured academic community and a succession (following a trail of job promotions for his editors) of mainstream commercial publishers; each establishment maintained a vested interest in representational literary art, as eminently teachable and saleable.

The words of approbation which course their way through John Barth's "Literature of Exhaustion" and "Literature of Replenishment" essays are "heroic," "salvation," "apotheosis," "virtuoso," and the like—terms which admittedly stand against the style of creative artists not aligned with either the academic or commercial entertainment industries of contemporary America. In his 1980 sequel, Barth recalled that his first essay was conceived and written on a university campus besieged by the challenging forces of demonstrating students and the reactions of tear-gassing police. It appears that he himself was quite uncomfortable in these circumstances, which others saw as genuinely revolutionary in terms of both curricular and aesthetic change. The key to Barth's personal aesthetic is back in that original essay written during the hectic days of the American 1960s, where he states his admiration for writers atypical of those times—that is, for writers who replace the representation of one action (an Aristotelian mimesis of behavior within the social world) with another: the act of writing a novel. *How that act is performed*, as an action in itself or as the representation of an action, is the key distinction in finding where Barth stands. Each of his examples, which include conventionally modernist works by Nabokov, Beckett, and Borges, are similar to his own, in that the typical suspension of disbelief in what one reads need not itself be suspended (as opposed to the anti-Aristotelian style of work the nonacademic writers were doing). "Novels which imitate the form of the Novel, by an author who imitates the role of the Author" are the books which Barth appreciates and writes himself. These booklength fictions—*Pale Fire, Labyrinths,* and *Giles Goat-Boy* are the cited examples—are written by admittedly good modernist writers who have held tenured positions in their own respective literary establishments. And each follows Aristotle's aesthetic belief that art imitates, rather than creates.

Literary works which suspend the suspension of disbelief, which in anti-Aristotelian fashion include the act of writing by the author and the act of reading by the reader as integral parts of their aesthetic, are excluded from John Barth's pantheon. He much prefers fictions which represent something already existing in the world—fictions in which the things that happen are metaphors for something else, not something in themselves. For Barth, it seems, fiction should forever be an imitation of an action, and not an action in itself.

This exclusion has unnecessarily complicated the history of late twentieth-century American literary art, for even among the Generation of '31 can be found excellent writers who alternately accept or reject the critical canon enshrined by received academic theory. The history of exhaustion and replenishment, however, has been a decidedly Aristotelian affair, and hence escapes the true spirit of our times. Yet Barth, like several other members of his literary generation, is capable of surprise; and his novel *Sabbatical* (New York: Putnam's, 1982), which follows his intellectual desk-clearing in *Letters* and "The Literature of Replenishment," is just the style of trans-mimetic work he had earlier resisted.

Sabbatical is aptly titled. Supposedly about a vacation retreat during which its man-and-wife narrators, after seven years of a second marriage, will take stock and determine future directions, the novel is in fact a reconstitution of Barth's technique in the wake of his first seven novels. As fiction in an age of criticism, it is productively self-conscious, with none of the awkward posing which marked *Giles Goat-Boy* and the works which followed. Its narrative situation comfortably accommodates talk about fiction writing without turning into self-reflexivity: co-narrator Fenn Turner had tried to be a novelist twenty years before, enrolling himself in the old-fashioned practices of authorship complete to a year holed up in Europe on a shoestring budget with nothing to do but write. But with nothing to do, nothing has resulted beyond metafiction of the most ill-considered type: "It was supposed to be about the politics of political journalism," Fenn recalls, "but it had taken an autobiographical turn and was more and more about a frustrated writer and a marriage strained by its first reciprocal adulteries" (p. 33). "The story, bogged down in self-concern, of a story bogged down in self-concern" (p. 42) is a deliberate parody of the Moebius strip style of fiction which obsessed Barth in his *Lost in the Funhouse* exercises. For *Sabbatical*, however, these memories have a more salutary effect, and his unfinished novel remains "the story of the story that taught me I couldn't write stories" (p. 44)—in the conventional sense, that is—and therefore it becomes a valid part of the new style of novel being composed before our eyes.

Fenn the failed novelist had become a CIA man, deciding to live a story because he feels he can't write one; but this very life of fiction offers the key to Barth's *Sabbatical*. As Fenn and his young wife, Susan, complete their half-year's cruise through the Caribbean and return to home port in Maryland, they shape their experiences into a story—a necessarily artificial act with its principles of composition and exclusion. By doing so, they recall adventures and fill each other in with their own memories, in the process treating the reader to a fully natural workshop session on narratology. Susan tells the story of her sister's torture and rape; Fenn fills in scenes from his first marriage; the happy circumstances of their meeting are recalled as well, so by novel's end the reader knows everything needed to appreciate their lives. They debate the contrary virtues of realism and fantasy, seeing the need for each. Myths and dreams are introduced for their structural services, and several of Barth's own stories and favorite notions (including the sperm-swim of "Night-Sea Journey" and the notion that "the key to the treasure is the treasure") are entertained.

What is being created, however, is their own narrative as their lives revolve about it, and in this case the key to the story is the story. As Fenn admires in Cervantes, the road is more comfortable than the inn. And as Susan, a scholar of nineteenth-century American literature and a descendent of Edgar Allan Poe (as Fenn is of Francis Scott Key) can explain, a compellingly interesting story such as *The Narrative of Arthur Gordon Pym* derives its effect from the fact that although the tale itself ends with the character's disappearance into the texture of narrative itself, its very telling testifies to his survival in its transmission. This life of fiction is what Susan and Fenn eventually find for themselves, amid the shambles of abortion, family dissolution, and vexing career decisions. As with *Pym*, "It is not that the end of the voyage interrupts the writing, but that the interruption of the writing ends the voyage"—and in an endless repetition of the tale, their writing never ends, since they "begin it at the end and end at the beginning" (p. 365). In this formulation, there is no imitation of imitation of reality. The fiction is most clearly and productively itself, making John Barth once more a timely representative of his literary age.

Ishmael Reed's Multicultural Aesthetic

THOSE DOUR GUARDIANS of official culture Ishmael Reed calls "high-ass Anglo critics" have always had trouble with his work, especially when they try to segregate facts from fiction. Even his partisans have rough going from time to time as they try to pigeonhole this writer who's built much of his career on the flamboyant eclipsing of stereotypes. Take a friend who's been wondering if he should zap poor Ishmael for being a "grant-hoarder" (the term is Reed's and he isn't one). This investigator's crowning argument is that among the contributors' notes to *Yardbird Lives!* (coedited with Al Young for Grove Press in 1978), Reed simply lists himself as "a businessman," as if admitting he's in league with the folks who run America's acronymic corporations and grants establishments.

"Hey wait," I beg my friend and cite Reed's disclaimer from the first page of his funniest novel, *The Last Days of Louisiana Red* (Random House, 1974), a note which warns that "in order to avoid detection by powerful enemies and industrial spies, nineteenth-century HooDoo people referred to their Work as 'The Business.'" The insipid grant-getting hustle my friend rightly condemns is hardly The Business our novelist describes, for if you read into *Louisiana Red* you'll find the HooDoo Businessmen have their own name for such she-nanigans every decent person would deplore: Moochism, as in Cab Calloway's "Minnie the Moocher." But for the victims of a monocultural education, artists like Calloway don't exist.

Businessman, HooDoo, Mama's Boy, High-Ass Anglo Critic—these are just a few of the words Ishmael Reed uses in both his essays and his fiction to articulate that odd confusion of history and imagination which so uniquely characterizes our times. Seeing how well his novel, *The Terrible Twos* (New York: St. Martin's, 1982), and essays collected in *God Made Alaska for the Indians* (New York: Garland, 1982) work togeth-er will help straighten out my grant-busting colleague, but it's worth remembering that Reed has been doing this for over two decades while the rest of us have been slowly catch-ing up. Take this description of "Dualism" from his *Catechism of d Neoamerican Hoodoo Church* (London: Paul Breman, 1970), a carefully articulated program of aesthetics masquerading as a book of poems:

> i am outside of
> history. i wish
> i had some peanuts, it
> looks hungry there in
> its cage
>
> i am inside of
> history. its
> hungrier than i
> thot   (p. 17)

In *The Terrible Twos*, Reed is supposedly outside of history; he sets his story in 1990, when the President is a former male model, the economy is worse than ever, and all that's left to trickle down is Christmas, which a bunch of power-hungry goons who run the country successfully buy and sell. *God Made Alaska for the Indians*, on the other hand, assembles eight essays and an afterword on environmentalists, Native Americans, literary politicians, prize fight promotions, male sexuality, race relations, the troubles in Ulster as seen by Irish-Americans, and the problems of multicultural artists—all of which deal directly with the demoralizing state of events since 1976 when Reed's last collection was assembled. But with an author like Reed in control, there's no real difference in subject or in method, and the result is a penetrating vision which by now surely ranks as the new decade's most insightful literary critique of American morals and manners.

It's at this intersection that the battle over Reed's work is fought: can the identity of history and imagination, just because our age apparently confuses them, be a valid method for the critique itself? For years, Reed has been complaining about the intellectual colonialism which judges American literature by nineteenth-century English and European standards—"all those books in rusty trunks," as he puts it, which by contrast make his own writing seem "muddled, crazy, and incoherent." In his attack on these old-order standards, Reed does disrupt some emotionally held ideals, but his genius is to base his method solidly within the multicultural American lower-middle class, which he claims is more ready to allow "the techniques and forms painters, dancers, film makers, and musicians in the West have taken for granted for at least fifty years, and the artists of other cultures for thousands of years." Hence, you'll find Reed talking about (and writing like) Cab Calloway, who since 1928 has never lacked a low-brow audience, black or white, rather than the intellectually uptown musicians more conventionally taken as models. You can also find him listening to Native Americans describing their two-century battle against Russian and American white men, where he quickly notes their method:

On the bombing of Angoon, another Tradition Bearer, George Davis, told me that in 1880 an American ship tried out a cannon-like gun and hit a whale. The whale leaped out of the ocean and "screamed like a wolf," he said as he told me a story part fiction, part autobiographical, part nonfiction (the new fiction is at least 20,000 years old). (P. 32)

Syncretism is one of the few formally abstract words in Reed's critical vocabulary, and he feels it is the key to a true national American literature reflecting the uniquely multicultural art which has evolved here. "Anglo" culture, as he calls it, then becomes one element among many, and the only loss is that of a dominant intellectual academy sworn to upholding the beliefs of a long-dead order. Gabriel García Marquez says much the same about his own multicultural, coastal Caribbean background where, as opposed to the rigidly colonial Spanish culture of the highlands capital in Bogotá, history and fiction were allowed to blend, making truth "one more illusion, just one more version of many possible vantage points" where "people change their reality by changing their perception of it." Within this aesthetic, fact and imagination become one. And as our present age has been shaped by this union, so Reed creates a common method for writing novels and essays by using the best of it while warning of its dangers when abused.

Both *The Terrible Twos* and *God Made Alaska for the Indians* are filled with Reed's customary mischief and fun. In the novel, President Dean Clift does things like helping sell merchandising rights to Santa Claus and declaring Adolf Hitler a posthumous American citizen, but balks when his advisors plan nuclear war with Nigeria as a way of wiping out the eco-

nomically "surplus people" on both sides. Meanwhile, back
in the quotidian reality of *God Made Alaska*, Reed's research
uncovers a "late nineteenth century American movement
called Teutonism" in which a serious politician "proposed a
way of ridding the land of both the unwelcome black and
Irish: 'Let an Irishman kill a Negro and get hanged for it'"
(p. 81). Both books are hilarious in their accounts of people
being swallowed by their own cultural signs, but things get
serious when Reed shows how dangerous a dead semiotics—
a code of social behavior deriving from discredited cultural
authority, such as monocultural white male dominance—can
be. Mama's boys, Daddy's girls: both the real and fictional
worlds suffer from them, and the biases of hot-sell TV and
high-powered establishment educations only make things
worse. There's a "scolding missionary tone" (p. 9) in the Sierra Club's attack on the Shee Atika tribes, and also a peculiar rhetoric to the presidential advice offered by *The Terrible
Twos'* wealthy Colorado brewer who boasts that "my family
has been making beer since they came through the Cumber-
land Pass with Dan Boone. They shot Injuns alongside Mor-
decai Lincoln and joined old Andy Jackson in his war against
the Seminoles" (p. 102). Why should this self-styled King of
Beer worry about the Native Americans his commercial development, Christmas Land, will drive from their Alaska
homes? "Injuns come and Injuns go," he blathers, "but Re-
gal Beer is here for eternity" (p. 102). Is monocultural America really this bad? Every paragraph in *God Made Alaska*
makes it seem worse, because Reed shows how it happens:

Native-American historians accuse Arthur Schlesinger, Jr., of
omitting any reference to the Trail of Tears of the Cherokee Nation
in his Pulitzer Prize-winning *The Age of Jackson*. Schlesinger, and
others, prepare for leadership people like Reverend Billy Moyers, a

former advisor to a President, who only recently found out that slavery wasn't merely the practice of some ignorant white trash overseers, but was endorsed by the judicial and legislative bodies of the time. His guest, A. Leon Higgenbottom, author of *In the Matter of Color*, was polite. He could have mentioned how American churches sold slaves to raise money to support their missionaries abroad, and how The American Government Sold Slaves to Raise Revenue!! (Pp. 6–7)

In our time, history and imagination are confused because there's been a king-hell conflict going on between two rival sign-making authorities, one authentic (the multicultural and nativistically American lower-middle class, which has invented jazz, blues, rock and roll, country swing, comic books, detective novels, fast food, and other items native to our shores) and the other a carry-over from a long-dead power (the European colonization, with its monocultural rhetoric and monological dictates). What can Reed do in these circumstances: write a counter-history of the Western world, as Khachig Tölölyan says Thomas Pynchon has done, exposing "the patriarchal and technological white West" while rallying for "the imposed-upon" who've been "inscribed with other peoples' meanings"? That's the negative side of his program, but our man Reed takes such positive joy in the real American culture which now and then wins a fight that Pynchon's solution seems fully unsatisfactory—there's too much joy to miss, both in exposing the phonies and giving credit for the good stuff.

God Made Alaska for the Indians is a commentary about being a necessary outsider to the monocultural elite. "Ishmael Reed?" some people will ask; "If he's not on the inside of our academic and publishing establishments, who is?" As if to answer, these eight essays range across contemporary America to indicate how one-sided and exclusionary its standards of cultural authority still are. And not just for black Americans. Reed's adversary vision is important because there is an entire national culture being systematically outlawed by an educational and media organization pledged to a set of ideals blind to what "nativistic" (meaning Afro-American, Hispanic-American, Oriental-American, even lower-middle-class Polish-American) literature is. "Here so long / We got spirit," Reed quotes the Alaskan-American poet Andy Hope, who like Reed has to keep laying down the challenge for attention: "Look me in the eye when I talk and you'll remember what I say" (p. 34).

Despite the great social turnabout in the 1960s which helped get Reed and other necessary outsiders rolling, official American culture is still very much a closed code. Roland Barthes would call it petit-bourgeois thinking, a dullish inability to image anything other than itself, but the crying shame is that here in America it is not even our own petit-bourgeois standard which is pulling down the blinds and locking the windows: it's a monocultural, monological, male-dominant and classically white European set of values which even as it died abroad took on an artifically new colonial life here. And despite all the radical social changes and curricular revisions, that attitude remains so strong as to be incessantly stifling, making contemporary studies a nuisance-ridden affair of having to continually struggle out from beneath the wet blanket of old, implacable cultural attitudes.

That's why Reed, whose "continuing autobiography of the mind" this collection is (following straight upon *Shrovetide in Old New Orleans* which was prefaced from the Alaska village where the new book's first essay begins), feels obliged to range from Sierra Club-Native American battles through the Ali-Spinks heavyweight championship bout and various linguistic, sexual, racial, and revolutionary topics to the book's

most impressive essay on the crazy spectacle of some displaced New York poets pumping a Buddhist revival in woolly
Colorado's Boulderado Hotel. Something, folks, is very
wrong out there, and Ishmael Reed is the practicing artist
and cultural theorist who can tell us why.

My interest in Reed's work is personal, a concern absolutely central to his arguments in *God Made Alaska*. Anyone
working on innovative American literature will inevitably
confront the same problems he outlines here, and Reed's essays are helpful because they explain so much of what has
been going haywire in our culture—for black writers, non-
elitists, Native Americans, and whoever else can't fit the establishment's Aristotelian and colonial standards. And we're
not talking about the trials of some foggy avant-garde.
Closed attitudes precede nativistically American work like
bad news moving in advance of a known troublemaker. In
1981, the editor of an ongoing literary encyclopedia wrote me
in desperation for a piece on Walter Abish, the novelist
who'd caught academia off guard by winning the first PEN/
Faulker prize—it turned out this editor couldn't find a single
scholar able "to comprehend Abish's work, let alone write
about it." In 1982, the publisher of a supposedly on-the-ball
San Francisco quarterly returned my essay on Richard Kostelanetz unread, saying he found it "impossible to deal with a
writer whose values and methods" he couldn't understand.
The pity is that this stuff has been going on, it seems, forever;
way back in 1976, Reed's *Yardbird 5* reprinted my even earlier
report of walking into what I'd hoped would be a wide-rang-
ing and open-minded literary gathering at San Francisco
State University and being accosted by an old-style Americanist who answered my friendly "Hello, I'm Jerry
Klinkowitz" with a rather hysterical and fully unprovoked
diatribe: "Ronald Sukenick! Ronald Sukenick! I can't read

him! I just can't read him!" Close behind was the department's top graduate student, pledged to a thesis on the academically acceptable Thomas Pynchon (a fine Aristotelian decked out in classically European values), chattering "Monkeys at typewriters! Monkeys at typewriters!" In this climate of self-professed illiteracy which characterizes so many English departments and publishing houses, there is not much one can answer back. Too often my own response has been to cash in my hand and call for pizza and beer. Reed, however, sticks around and fights, armed with a finely articulated brief against this claustrophobic set of cultural rules.

Reed's stature is, in part, measured by the greatness of his enemies, and in *God Made Alaska* he finds himself aligned against the entire Anglo establishment which disparages anything outside colonial culture, from the blues to cowboy novels (just two of the notable art forms unique to our shores). There is a very definite anti-American mindset to these constrictive attitudes; in one of the very first critical histories of our country's writing, *The Spirit of American Literature* (New York: Dodd, Mead and Co., 1911), Bostonian John Macy postulated that "in literature nationality is determined by language rather than by blood or geography" as a way of justifying his claim that "American literature is a branch of English literature, as truly as are English books written in Scotland or South Africa" (p. 3). Nobody would be so outrageous as to go on record with that specific claim today, but the spirit behind it sets the rules by which culture gets funded, published, and taught. Lower-middle-class Americans of all ethnic backgrounds are taxed to support a European-culture-oriented tradition of grand opera, symphony, and ballet they will never see or hear, even if they wanted to. When the environmentalists of the Sierra Club present their claims to

Native American land, Reed notes that "they often used arguments which sounded similar to the Romanov's appeal to divine rights. The rest of us lacked 'qualifications.' We didn't meet their 'standards'" (p. 4). The methods of "colonizing" Alaskan tribes in the nineteenth century, "naturalizing" them at the century's turn, or locking up their assets for "the national interest" now, Reed shows, are all based on the same monocultural arrogance that proclaims white male standards as the only ones with value.

By these same terms, a black heavyweight champion of the world becomes the unimaginable Other, the role Ken Norton was obliged to play in *Mandingo* and *Drum*: "The women want to ball him, and the men want to do battle with him; some people want to do both" (p. 39). So much for official cultural standards, which an innovative champ like Muhammad Ali can subvert by going directly to the people whom the establishment has counted out more subtly but no less effectively: "He is more effective because he speaks to Americans in American images, images mostly derived from comic books, television, and folklore. To be a good black poet in the 60s meant capturing the rhythms of Ali and Malcolm X on the page. . . . His prose is derived from the trickster world of Bugs Bunny and Mad Comics" (pp. 43–44). Reed identifies a further split between official and authentic culture in his challenge to Dick Cavett and John Simon on the issue of "Black English." How can it be "eradicated," Cavett asks and Simon implores. "You'd have to eradicate the black people" is the obvious linguistic answer, which Reed finds a "chilling thought, considering that there are historical precedents for people being exterminated because they didn't speak and write the way others thought they should" (p. 67). But more practically, Reed adds, there is a crucial difference between the received language of official culture (which is by definition drained of personal imagination for the purposes of "doing business" smoothly) and the way people within the culture actually think, speak, and feel:

You not gone make me give up Black English. When you ask me to give up my Black English you askin me to give up my soul. But for everyday reasons of commerce, transportation-hassleless mobility in everyday life, I will talk to 411 in a language both the operator and I can understand. I will answer the highway patrolman who stops me, for having a broken rear light, in words he and I both know. The highway patrolman, who grew up on Elvis Presley, might speak Black English at home, because Black English has influenced not only blacks but whites too. (P. 68)

Right there is the issue: for mundane points of information, free of characterizing value, official language will have to do. But in terms of artistic expression and communication, where culture's lasting business takes place, there is another, nativistically American language which gets systematically discounted by the "King's English" crowd which insists that the discourse of novels, plays, and poems be conducted in the same tongue, now so stiffly formal because it represents a culture which died one hundred years ago on a land mass three thousand miles away. And because the real American culture is kept at home behind closed doors, the marketplace language is itself never transformed, and so through no free choice of their own white cops find themselves speaking to black citizens in an outmoded language formed by structures of colonial authority bearing small relation to the lives they personally lead. Richard Ohmann's *English in America* made this point nearly ten years ago, but Freshman Writing standards remain those of nineteenth century England because that's from where our official culture derives its values.

Stale images, such as the black-male-as-rapist, come from stale thinking, and Reed shows how there is easy money to be made from traffic in such worthless symbols. Meanwhile the real issue is deliberately ignored, for "the most lethal macho is white macho, since white men have the extravagant means with which to express it. If the nuclear button is pushed, it will, no doubt, be pushed by a finger belonging to a white male. While black macho might be annoying, white male macho could be the death of us" (p. 73). But the official culture "reads white," having "more regard for whites in Europe than for nonwhites in America" (p. 77) simply because the old standards of judgment point in that direction. When a culture is so isolated from its everyday personal language and values, it atrophies. Hence, Reed's well-meaning desire to "stir up some mischief" which at least shakes open a few minds and closes a few mouths: "Ethnic purity. White superiority. The Nazis were doing in the streets what some white Liberal Arts departments preach elsewhere." Or even more tellingly, he suggests to an MLA meeting "that certain characteristics of blacks in novels written by white liberal intellectuals reminded me of the Nazi caricatures of their victims. A commotion ensued. I thought I was going to have to slug my way out of the hall" (p. 79). But as he learns from the Irish Republicans speaking at their own cultural center, "the victors will not be those who inflict most, but those who endure the most" (p. 99).

At times in the past Reed's stridency has cost him part of his audience, but the gentler fun of *Twos* and *Alaska* is calculated to open some minds even as it closes some mouths. The egoless self-apparency of his method, based as it is on the common language and sentiment of most Americans far away from the intellectual centers, virtually guarantees this;

for when Reed simply "sits back and takes it all in" as the monocultural aristocrats hang themselves with their own devoluted chatter, how can you help but take his side? The emotional two-year-olds of his novel are their own worst enemies; there's no need for the author to turn the knife in them as he's been tempted to do in earlier novels. In *Alaska*'s most conclusive essay, "American Poetry: Is There a Center?", watch Reed stare in disbelief as Michael Brownstein pumps him with the information that "the hottest scene in the country was taking place in Boulder," which thanks to the Naropa Institute's presence in the Colorado hills has made the place an "energy center." A few months before, the smart boys had been telling Reed that all the action was just north of San Francisco Bay, but his checking revealed that their idea of the source, Bolinas, "was a mere watering hole for international artists, intellectuals, and people who grew up in households with five maids" (p. 105). So now he sits listening to this academic enthusiast "who sometimes looks like a guy who wore a prep school cap and shorts at one time" claiming that Boulder's where it's at. Whose side are you on through all of this? Where do you think "the center for American poetry" might really be? At the essay's end, far from the circus in Colorado (described with merciless accuracy), Reed finds his answer: "In every poet's heart."

Monology works in curious ways, and Reed can speak his mind without slandering Brownstein, who he quickly admits is a good and thoughtful poet. It's the system, Reed advises, which makes this transplanted Tennessean sound so bad: "People in centers see themselves as the center because they can't see the whole scene with an eye for detail" (p. 120). Reed's ideal, which is a lot closer to the American reality which lies beyond the suffocating pale of Manhattan, Boulder, and Bolinas, is one of multicultural syncretism—of a truly national literature which can absorb radically different contributions and come out stronger for it. But the old system of "pledged allegiance to Anglo culture" still dominates the news media, publishing, and education. Idi Amin is everyone's favorite black ruler; alternatives to white culture in America are discussed by CBS on the level of "tacos and watermelons", plus "there was that sad issue of *Partisan Review* (44, no. 2 [1977]) called 'New York and National Culture: An Exchange,' in which a panel of New York intellectuals claimed to represent National Culture when in reality they sounded like village people whispering about haunted houses" (p. 114). Like the Romanovs, those who've assumed they hold divine rights do not change roles easily.

What Reed calls the Anglo establishment thrives on dead signs, cliches of a once-living culture which now misdirect and deplete our country's imaginative energy. Therefore, his first job is to expose this state of affairs and then to bring our language and its signs back to life as self-apparent realities. *God Made Alaska for the Indians* does this for the history we've shared since 1976, and *The Terrible Twos* takes further license to push the argument through fiction. All systems are fictions, our times have taught us, and fictions in turn create functional realities. Reed likes to demonstrate how the folks in control manipulate us—that's the wickedly funny part. Ishmael Reed triumphs as an American writer when he seizes the oppressor's tools and forges his own reality: a perception of disparate forces brought together in a single complex vision which is clearly superior, based as it is on a broader range of seeing and expressing. Consider what the media and the police made of Patty Hearst's kidnapping by the Symbionese Liberation Army, and how Reed's method pulls it all together:

The security problem. From the early revolts there had always been the security problem. Even Gullah Jack couldn't protect Vesey from it. The American Secret Police has caused conflict between the Black Panthers and the United States; bugged Huey Newton's apartment; but the SLA brought out the Keystone in them. They flaunted their presence before the authorities, creating an arabesque American myth involving Patty Hearst and Cinque. Arabian nights of California, the rich white girl and her genie; the Dragon has come. Visionary hostage-takers, Artaud's mad actors, burning up on television. Now the psychodramatic politician was on the scene. One man, no leaks, unless he's schizoid and rats on himself. The first time rebellion could achieve a force equal to the opponents of rebellion. Eight thousand tons of plutonium were missing. Who had them? Enough to make 80 A-bombs. (P. 90)

What a way to live, but that's what much of our culture has turned out to be, as rival sign-making systems fight it out in books and films and on records and TV. Like *God Made Alaska for the Indians, The Terrible Twos* is much more than a simple counter-history: quoting a penitent Nelson Rockefeller from the lowest circle of Hell and playing with some off-the-record apocrypha about his death from a group of corporate scoundrels, Reed can pull together the many different and contradictory levels of our contemporary American "truth" and give us a persuasive account of how we live today. Reed the novelist and essayist is a careful semiotic researcher who, once he's done the hard work of running up and down the stairs for facts, gives language free play to project itself into previously unexplored corners of public experience, lighting up some truths which those afflicted with cultural tunnel vision might otherwise never see.

Yet official standards remain belligerently exclusive and reductively stereotypical: "It's too bad that the different cultures which go to make up American civilization are communicating only on the tacos and watermelons level" (p. 125). Such proscriptions only weaken the parties who make them;

for, as Reed argues, "the drive against integrating schools being waged by some oily politicians is regrettable since it's the white students who really need it if they are to survive in a complicated, multicultural world" (pp. 125–26). Who suffers most? "It is the white students who are being culturally suffocated because even black C students have it over them; they're bicultural, and the hispanic students are tricultural." But the ugliness and viciousness of an official culture, Aristotelian in its aesthetic and colonialistic in its ethic, for the most part prevails. "At this time in American history," Reed concludes, "we are like ghosts talking gibberish through different dimensions, and stupid men do not make good mediums" (p. 126).

John Irving's World According to Fiction

EARLY IN *THE WATER-METHOD MAN* (New York: Random House, 1972), John Irving presents a biographical sketch of his protagonist, Fred "Bogus" Trumper. Born March 2, 1942, in New Hampshire, and educated at Phillips Exeter, the Universities of Pittsburgh, New Hampshire (lettering in wrestling), Vienna (studying German), and Iowa (graduate school), Trumper's life is a model of the author's own. Through all five of Irving's novels, there runs a constant thread of autobiography—not always of the fact-to-fact variety, but of a more abstractly compositional nature, as unique elements of John Irving's life are shuffled through various combinations to create the essential style of his fiction.

Trained bears, for instance—nearly every novel has one, as a suggestion of life's pathos and mute humiliation. For quaint obsolescence, there's the remarkable car, a 1954 Zorn-Witwer (featuring a horizontal gear-shift column pulled out of the dash) which appears in all five books, as does Vienna itself, that nineteenth-century museum of a city for which the author has such fondness. And it's a very special

Vienna, including the same apartment at Schwindgasse 15/2, in the fourth district, although from novel to novel it's inhabited by widely different sets of characters. Each novel has much of its action set in Maine or New Hampshire, but also—for contrast—in Iowa, where Irving both studied and later taught. And, of course, there are the Austrian scenes. What's amazing is not how often these elements reappear, but how few of them there are for so many key repetitions. The effect is to establish a familiarity from book to book, and to stamp each as the unmistakable work of John Irving, whose own life has turned on this same point.

There's one other repetition, unusual for Irving because it is not a place or object but a person, and how he is used helps explain the more characteristic biographical references. In both *The Water-Method Man* and Irving's next novel, *The 158-Pound Marriage* (New York: Random House, 1974), there appears a minor character named Helmbart, a proponent of "the new novel." An obvious play on the occasional duo-syllabic pronunciation of Donald Barthelme's last name, Helmbart is described as a metafictional writer along the lines of Barthelme, John Barth, and William H. Gass. In *The Water-Method Man*, Helmbart is present simply through his novel *Vital Telegrams*, which is cited as a structural model for Ralph Packer's avant-garde film on Bogus Trumper's life. The later novel introduces Helmbart in person, as the writer-in-residence at the main characters' college, where he and his fiction are heartily disliked. The narrator and his friends "agreed that when the subject of fiction became how to write fiction, we lost interest; we were interested in prose, surely, but not when the subject of the prose became prose itself" (p. 72). Irving takes such a dislike to Helmbart and his artistic methods that he indulges in a bit of metafiction himself, running the poor man through a mill of embarrassing pratfalls until he's purged from the action and Irving's novel can continue with its more life-oriented dance of trained bears, antique cars, and other familiar scenes from Austria, Iowa, and Maine.

John Irving's objection to Helmbart's work and his contrary method in his own establishes the central purpose of Irving's art: that fiction cannot be *just* about the act or theory of writing, but must incorporate the act or theory into a fiction that's still about life. His favorite writer is Charles Dickens, who balanced sentimentality with the attractive and persuasive powers of life itself. "As a writer it is cowardly to so fear sentimentality that one avoids it altogether," Irving has complained in his essay on Dickens, "In Defense of Sentimentality" (*New York Times Book Review*, 25 November 1979, p. 3). The result is an unaffordable loss of human interest. "A short story about a four-course meal from the point of view of a fork will never be sentimental," Irving writes. "It may never matter very much to us either" (p. 96). In other essays and interviews, he has reemphasized his point that fiction stripped of human sentiment is literature devoid of life.

Helmbart, then, is somewhat of an anti-talisman for John Irving, who conducts a polemic against this "new novelist" both in person and in theory. In *The Water-Method Man*, filmmaker Ralph Packer compares his own improbable artistic doings to Helmbart's method in *Vital Telegrams*, the jacket of which attests: "The transitions—all the associations, in fact—are syntactical, rhetorical, *structural*; it is almost a story of sentence structure rather than of characters; Helmbart complicates variations on forms of sentences rather than plot" (pp. 243–44). The narrator pronounces *Vital Telegrams* to be unreadable; Ralph Packer has proclaimed that structure is all, but Helmbart's way of handling it leaves John Irving cold. Yet again there is a hedging of the bet. Just as the

author took metafictional pleasure in humiliating his creation in *The 158-Pound Marriage* (recalling the fun Gilbert Sorrentino had in *Imaginative Qualities of Actual Things* with characters he dislikes), the method of Helmbart's *Vital Telegrams*
serves as the model for Ralph Packer's film, *Fucking Up*—
which is the story of Trumper's life. In Fred Trumper's
actual life story, structure is indeed all, for the novel's thirty-
eight short chapters (and the film's quickly crosscut scenes)
jump back and forth among four distinct geographical locations and many more separate time schemes. The essence of
the story is to be found in the structure of its relations rather
than in any discursive survey of character. But Irving's method is not Helmbart's (nor Barth's or Barthelme's), for the
points of structural relationship are not mere factors of syntax but are instead the humanly appealing elements of his
character's lives, from trained bears and Zorn-Witwers to the
places Irving has lived.

The Water-Method Man, by far the most complex of John
Irving's novels, is his laboratory for testing out the syntax of
his protagonist's life, which is so confused that a clarifying
grammar of relationships remains a constant challenge.
"Her gynecologist recommended him to me," it begins, from
the very start in a complex and indirect manner, which is
compounded by the next fact, that "the best urologist in New
York is French" (p. 3). Fred Trumper is at the doctor's because of a nonspecific ailment, a seemingly incurable infec-
tion due to the "narrow, winding road" (p. 5) of his urinary
tract which is unable to flush out common bacteria. What's
needed is a corrective operation, to literally straighten
Trumper out, but he resists. Throughout his life he has
avoided endings, whether it is following his father's advice
and choosing a specialized career, or completing his doctoral
dissertation, a translation of the Old Low Norse epic, *Akthelt*

and Gunnel. The unpleasantness of facing an operation is obvious enough, and the grim nature of his Norse saga offers little encouragement. Trumper shows one stanza as an example:

> Gunnel loved to look at Akthelt.
> His knife was so long.
> But she knew in her heart
> The world was too strong.

At this point he stops translating. "The world *is* too strong," he admits, "I saw everything coming!—the author was trying to foreshadow the inevitable doom! Clearly Akthelt and Gunnel were headed for grief. I knew, and I simply didn't want to see it out" (p. 22).

Trumper's inability to face conclusions along his life's winding road provides a structure for *The Water-Method Man* which never leaves the narrative at rest. Four actions take place simultaneously: being married and going to graduate school in Iowa City, filmmaking in New York's Greenwich Village, looking for his old friend Merrill Overturf in Vienna (with assorted flashbacks to earlier times in Austria), and visiting his friend Couth in Maine. Complementing all four geographies is the saga of Akthelt and Gunnel, which Trumper finds easier to invent than to translate; its developments are henceforth keyed off the continuing events in his own life. And that life is quadruply fragmented. In Iowa he is a student, husband, and father, struggling to pay the bills and keep his family intact; New York finds him living with another woman, his studies forsaken as he tries to regain control of things through filmmaking; the Austrian scenes are chaotic, thanks to the irresponsible model of behavior offered by Merrill Overturf; Maine, however, is secure and idyllic, because of the stabilizing presence of his more reliable friend, Couth. And counterposed to each of these narrative lines runs the doomed saga of his Old Low Norse characters, written in a tongue from which no modern languages developed, the deadest language of them all.

Each location is strongly characterized by the type of detail for which Irving is famous. Indeed, a few key elements are repeated so often as to become narrative fetishes, distinctively anchoring the story line and providing a measure for the novel's progress. In Iowa, this marker is Mr. Fitch, Fred Trumper's friendly retired neighbor who's forever out raking his lawn and is hence privileged to observe Trumper's unending foibles. "*Scritch-scritch*," comes the familiar sound of Mr. Fitch, whom Trumper characterizes as "the grim raker." Even at midnight the old gentleman is roused awake by the sound of another leaf crashing against his lawn. Like time itself, Fitch is ever-present, a sign of the deadening mortality of Iowa life which Trumper must eventually escape.

Although the novel opens in New York, at the urologist's office, most of Irving's early chapters take place in Iowa City, where the day-to-day humiliations of student poverty establish his story's comic nature. The house Trumper rents is falling apart, its screens pushed out and the toilet plugged with the refuse of last summer's renters. His wife, Biggie, is shamed at the grocery store, where the manager won't accept her check; and one memorable chapter consists of twelve highly personalized letters to creditors, constructing artful dodges and creative excuses for not paying their bills. Through it all, Fred Trumper identifies with the underdog and sees his own perilous condition as similar to that of the mouse Biggie is trying to trap in the basement. Each night Trumper sneaks down the stairs to spring the mousetrap. "Don't be frightened," he tells the little rodent. "I'm on *your* side" (p. 55).

A year later, but in a chapter that's adjacent thanks to the novel's syntactically cubist structure, Trumper is seen in New York, worrying over a small tropical fish that's been eaten by its larger colleagues: "Trumper slammed his hand hard on the water surface; the other fish bolted, fled in terror, collided with each other and glanced off the surface of the glass walls. 'You bastards!' Trumper screamed, 'Which one of you did it?' He stared fiercely at them, the lean yellow one with a blue fin, the evil-red one. He stabbed into the tank with a pencil" (p. 82). Here in New York Trumper is living with another woman, Tulpen, and is working for another project director, Ralph Packer. But he is no more stable with her than with his wife in Iowa, and he shows as little determination to complete the film as he did to finish his thesis. Tulpen from time to time suggests having a baby, but for Trumper this is a *direction*, which would lead to an *ending*, and for the structure of his life such devices are unthinkable.

The scenes in Austria help explain Fred Trumper's condition. Twelve chapters of the book's thirty-eight, alternating between New York and Iowa, precede "Remember Merrill Overturf?" which introduces Trumper's friend and his first trip abroad. Characteristically, this section is introduced by one of the novel's set pieces of slapstick action, Trumper's skiing lesson on the children's slope, an adventure whose mayhem reflects the disorganization of Trumper's life. Having left Biggie, Trumper flies to Vienna in search of his old undergraduate roommate. "I prefer to fall to pieces abroad" (p. 200), he tells his dissertation director, quoting a line from *Akthelt and Gunnel* which he has actually written himself. Through six months of searching, most of which takes place in a drugged haze, Overturf cannot be found. But as is typical in John Irving's world of fiction, certain key elements remain the same, such as an encounter with the odd little man of no determinate language ("*Grajak ok bretzet . . . gra, gra, gra!*") whom Trumper answers in Old Low Norse: "Bogus thought that it had been like a conversation with Mr. Fitch" (pp. 226–27).

Dominating the Austrian chapters, which number only seven out of the novel's thirty-eight but which are spaced at intervals between Chapters 12 and 35, is the character Merrill Overturf. A strong influence on Trumper's life, Overturf is often recalled in chapters otherwise set in Iowa, New York, or Maine. "Merrill Overturf and other irregular people are unsuited to conditions demanding careful routines" (p. 208), Trumper notes, confirming his affinity for this friend whose life resists direction and conclusions as does his own. Merrill's winsomely reckless conduct is a constant temptation away from the duties of Iowa, the lessons of New York, or the promises of resolution in Maine. "He was the great illusion of my life," Trumper can admit: "That such a self-destroying fool can be so indestructible" (p. 114). For much of his life, Merrill Overturf careens along a narrow route between insulin reaction and alcohol poisoning, seemingly immune to the physical dangers he so recklessly courts. Hence the shock when Trumper's six-month search turns up Merrill dead. Merrill's own grand illusion has been the presence of a German tank at the bottom of the Danube, sunk through the ice by partisans during the last month of the war. He has enchanted Trumper with the story, and also uses it to charm young women he picks up at American Express. Swimming out one night to find it, he drowns. "She hadn't believed him," the girlfriend testifies, a fact which Trumper immediately relates to Merrill's Peter-Pan-like existence. "'I would have believed you,' Bogus Trumper said aloud" (p. 268).

And so Vienna, in all its deadly confusion, is abandoned as a lapsed dream. From here, Trumper makes the first of several returns to Maine and his boyhood friend Couth. "Couth, I can't tell you how glad I am to see you," Trumper exclaims. "Here you are saving my life again. . . . You're the one fixed star in the heavens, Couth!" (p. 281). Couth as a person and Maine as a location each speak for the comfort of routine, a secure quality which Trumper's life in Iowa, New York, and Vienna has lacked. Routine is something Trumper can appreciate if not practice himself, as he admires the scene from his Norse saga where the warrior king Akthelt ritualistically girds himself for battle while his wife Gunnel improvises her own striptease routine to keep him home.

On his second-last visit, Trumper discovers that life in Maine has gone on placidly without him, to the extent that his role as husband and parent has been assumed by Couth. Biggie murmurs for Couth, and not Trumper, in her sleep, while his son Colm enjoys a fatherly companionship he's never had in Iowa. "Bogus thought, A routine. Colm has a routine. How kids love a good routine. Did *I* ever establish a routine with Colm?" (p. 291). These scenes of paternal displacement are especially difficult for Trumper, who has been fearful for his child's safety. Couth has always envied Trumper his "offspring," and does seem better adjusted to handle the responsibility. Trumper, however, is all paranoia:

"But with children, it's different," I said, not knowing how to explain what was so different. I once wrote Merrill about it. I said that children gave you a sudden sense of your own mortality, which was clearly something that Merrill Overturf had no sense of; he never answered me. But I simply meant that you noticed how your priorities had changed. For example, I used to like motorcycles; I couldn't ride one after Colm was born. I don't think it was just responsibility; it's just that children give you a sense of time. It was as if I'd never realized how time moved before. (P. 144)

Trumper wants to secure his son in a "simulated natural habitat," to which Couth objects as "pasturing." But Couth needs no artificial pastures because he is peacefully content. This sense of resolution evades Trumper, however, until the very end, which takes place most suitably in Maine.

What Fred Trumper has instead of peace and contentment is aptly described in three set-piece narratives distributed throughout the center of Irving's book. Chapter 11, "Notre Dame 52, Iowa 10," finds Trumper at his part-time job of selling football souvenirs outside the Hawkeyes' stadium and trying to hide from his young language student, Lydia Kindle. The first half of Chapter 13, "Remember Merrill Overturf?", features the Austrian skiing incident. The longest and most complex set piece occurs as Chapter 18, "One Long Mother of a Day," during which Trumper botches a seduction of Miss Kindle and limps back to Iowa City for even more troubles. These three chapters establish the novel's comic tone but are more important in a structural sense: as microcosmic reflections of the book's larger patterns, they show the reader how the narrative in general will proceed—a direction which otherwise might be too elusive with each chapter jumping from place to place and from time to time. Moreover, they give a clue to Trumper's culpability, helping to explain why everything he touches goes wrong. Some of the novel's chapters are narrated in the third person—all nine of the Maine scenes, for example. There is occasional use of second person direct address as well, such as when Trumper composes imaginary letters to Biggie. But these three antic episodes are told in the first person, and seeing Trumper's mind at work reveals the pathology of his disorganized life.

"Notre Dame 52, Iowa 10" begins with a simple setting of the scene—the hapless business of selling Hawkeye regalia during a losing season. Into this circumstance, where Trumper is already at his weakest, comes the chapter's catalyst: the fetching Miss Lydia Kindle, upon whom Trumper has designs, and her "utter *Glork* of a boyfriend" (the term is Old Low Norse, a symptom of Trumper's identification of his own life's narrative with the epic he is forging). Trumper is embarrassed and hides beneath his sales stand; the boyfriend thinks it is abandoned and steals a team button, and in so doing pulls the stand and Trumper down upon himself.

From the start, it is obvious that Trumper has the talent for making and then compounding his own troubles. He has no business lusting after the innocent Miss Kindle in the first place, and hiding from her and her boyfriend only makes his eventual discovery all the more humiliating. In textual terms, Trumper is a machine who generates complications, and even in the shame of his pratfall he finds the chance to spice things up a bit by lapsing into Old Low Norse as the *Glork* struggles out from beneath the collapsed stand and sprawling vendor:

> "*Klegwoerum*," I tell her. "*Vroognaven okthelm abthur, awf?*"
> She gawks while the board struggles under me. I change my language and garble German up to Lydia: "*Wie gehts dir heute? Hoffentlich gut.*" (P. 61)

As narrator, Trumper can further color the action through his choice of descriptive language, such as when "the *Glork* scuttles out from under my fallen wares looking like a little crushed crab" (p. 62).

To keep things moving, Irving alternates Trumper's colorful language with a further batch of catalysts. The head concessionaire walks into the scene and further embarrasses Trumper; a crowd forms to deride the hassled vendor, a scene he enhances through further description ("The crowd is thinking, after a crowd's fashion, Now if they would only put on something like this during the half. If only they displayed the vendors, fed them to Iowa hogs, let them humbly try to defend themselves with their goofy showboards," (p. 64). Making things worse, as is his habit, Trumper charges through the crowd, trampling spectators and completely destroying his salesboard.

The scene concludes more quietly, with what will become a common Trumper routine: self-discovery, from which one would think he'd learn a collective lesson, but then a mistaken discovery by Biggie, who gets the facts all wrong and sets Trumper off again down the slapstick course of his long and winding road. "But see me!," he is shocked to admit when glimpsing his ragged self in a store window. "My hair is wild, my eyes are mad, my mouth is uncontrollably grinning; my face is a grimace, as tight-skinned and as blotchy as a clenched fist" (p. 68). Lydia Kindle has followed him offering comfort, and for once it seems poor Trumper will face up and go straight. But when he limps home to Biggie, all she can see is Lydia's lipstick on his cheek. "'You bastard!' said Biggie, and brought up from the pail a soggy cleaning rag, first swatting my face with it, then wiping it across my mouth. Perhaps it was the ammonia that started my eyes watering, with those fumes so strong under my nose" (p. 69). Colm wanders in to find his father not a beacon of strength but another helpless creature in need of mothering. The only self-knowledge gained from all of this is Trumper's determination that in any place or circumstance he'd never succeed. The chapter closes with him ready for his next mistake.

The skiing lesson which begins Chapter 13, "Remember Merrill Overturf?", is more harmlessly comic, thanks to Trumper's ability to characterize events in terms of humorously transformative language and slapstick behavior. From a simple situation—climbing up the towrope on the scaled-down children's slope—Trumper manages to generate a full chapter's action. He can't bend low enough to keep the rope level, and so stands straight, pulling up the kids with him. "Above me I saw the little children, their skis completely off the ground, hanging from the rope, swinging like little puppets." Some fall off in his path, and Trumper's reaction is innocent: "I was surprised at how cleverly I kept my balance as I skied over my first child" (p. 84). What follows is almost entirely a product of Trumper's language and his framing of perspective. The little kids call for help and cry for their mothers in German—naturally, since this is Austria, but comic in Trumper's reportorial use of a foreign language; by distancing the children from us, he makes their fate less tragic and more harmlessly laughable. Language reestablishes their innocence on the downhill slope and protects them from harm; as Trumper describes it, "Larkish little children flew by us, poling and zigzagging and falling as lightly and safely as little wads of wool." Unable to slalom, Trumper soon speeds out of control, but still maintains his comic pose (Merrill calls for him to fall down—"In front of the children? Never"). As he hurtles down the slope, "the lift line broke up; spectators and skiers burst for cover. I imagined an air raid, from the point of view of the bomb" (p. 85). In the midst of this hysteric action, Trumper is comically calm and calculating, especially as he reaches the looming snowbank which ends the course. "The surprise has rarely been equalled," he quietly notes, "to discover that skis can climb." From this site of impending devastation, Trumper shifts his narrative focus to the scene below, "a family of sturdy Germans getting out of their Mercedes." Again, the comedy is achieved through caricature: "Father Round in stout lederhosen knickers and a feathered Tyrolean hat; Mother Heft in hiking boots and swinging a walking stick with an ice-ax point; children: Dumpling, Dumpier, and Dollop." Even after he crashes into them, he manages to prolong the narrative, noting that "Father Round. . . . quickly scanned the skies, no doubt looking for the *Luftwaffe*" (p. 86). As in the football chapter, a crowd gathers to deride the hapless Trumper, and again the action closes with a misconstrued implication. "We've missed the first event," a just-arriving woman complains. "Madame," Merrill corrects her as he drags the battered Trumper away, "be glad the first event missed *you*" (p. 87).

"One Long Mother of a Day," covering twenty-three pages and the book's longest chapter, repeats the plan of Trumper's earlier set-piece narrations and replicates the novel's structure as a whole. "It begins, actually, the night before, with an argument, wherein Biggie accuses Merrill Overturf of childish, escapist pranksterism and further claims that I have been able to heroize Merrill only because he has been missing from my life for so long" (p. 157), Trumper explains. His behavior in all three episodes has been irresponsibly antic along these lines, recalling his characterization of Merrill as the "great illusion" of his life. Typically, this adventure gets underway with a failure to face authority, now personified as his father; prompted to phone him and protest his disinheritance, the timid son is unable to speak, leading Dr. Trumper to believe the call is from a patient in trauma.

Fred Trumper never says a word, but the next day undertakes a sequence of actions which accomplishes even more havoc. Meeting Lydia Kindle in the library parking lot, he coaxes her into a countryside drive, bent on seduction. But his characterization of the scene dissuades him: all he can think of is her avenging family, and once he begins to undress her the childlike underthings she wears remind him of vulnerable little Colm. "I shut my eyes in her powdered cleavage, noting a sort of candy musk," he prompts himself. "But why does my mind run to slaughterhouses, and to all the young girls raped in wars?" (p. 166). Trumper can manage neither his language, nor his imagination which creates it—he is a text-producing machine running out of control—and just as his inclination for the lowly comic led to such trouble in the football and skiing scenes, now the words and images in which he chooses to narrate the seduction scene confound his intentions. He's unable to perform; Lydia feels rejected and humiliated, and pushes him naked from the car. As in the previous episodes, Trumper at once visualizes the epic consequences: "*He died of exposure on the duck-flown shores of the Coralville Reservoir!*" (p. 167).

As is typical in Trumper's narrations, the offbeat end of one action simply begins another; there are no resolutions in his life, as yet. Hobbling through the stubbled bean fields and down a country road, naked except for his condom, he typically encounters an audience, in this case two duck hunters who, after voicing their disbelief, help retrieve his clothes and drive him into Iowa City, giving him as a memento a gutted, half-plucked duck. Dropped across from married student housing on laundry day, Trumper once again parades before an allegorical audience, this time including "Mrs. Sheet." He runs into Ralph Packer and tries to shrug off his situation: "Why, it's Bogus Trumper, out walking his duck" (p. 173). Language games and comic implications keep the scene going, as Ralph worries "What if that duck has friends?" (p. 175). When Trumper finally drags himself home, it is only to initiate more troubles which await him like his universal fate: Mr. Fitch spots him sneaking in the cellar door with the battered duck, and Trumper's first move in the dark is a barefoot step into the freshly baited mousetrap. For her part, Biggie is willing to prolong the action with more duck jokes ("Give it brandy. . . . Perhaps we can revive it"), but when his rush for the bathroom to urinate is thwarted by the still in-place condom which bulges out like an expanding balloon,

Biggie again misreads the essentials of Trumper's oddball situation. Colm appears on cue, happily wandering off with the duck ("*May he remember me as the father with fancy presents of all kinds*") just as the doorbell rings to announce a special delivery letter:

> The mailman entered, waving a letter. It happened so suddenly that he startled Colm, who shrieked back down the hall, dragging the duck after him. I waddled three more painful knee steps to the kitchen door, still clutching my balloon, and rolled out of sight into the kitchen.
>
> "Special delivery! Special handling!" the mailman announced again flatly—not having been forwarned of the possibility that he might ever be in need of a more appropriate remark. (P. 179)

The letter is from his father, a communication which concludes the scene exactly where it has begun. But for Trumper there is no resolution, for the $5,000 check enclosed—intended as a student loan—simply provides the means for escape. The next day he's off to Vienna, in search of Merrill Overturf, the reckless illusion which has kept his entire life off track.

Within these set-piece narratives, Irving has codified the structure both of Fred Trumper's lifestyle and the system by which his own novel is organized. Each adventure begins with an embarrassing situation which Trumper's reaction only makes worse. Indeed, his ability to keep reacting, to continue improvising with the materials of slapstick comedy, keeps each chapter running far beyond logical limits. After a point, the bulk of each narrative's action is taking place in language rather than event; time may run out and the story's material may exhaust itself, but Trumper's imagination keeps producing, characterizing events in terms guaranteed to compound his problems.

Helmbart's *Vital Telegrams* was organized on the principle of syntactic, rhetorical, and above all structural associations, and although John Irving's narrator explicitly disavows the metafictional nature of this approach, the various elements of *The Water-Method Man* are joined together according to a similar syntactic design. Chapters are linked together both externally and internally. Between Chapters 4 and 5 this linkage is thanks to the word *insomniac* which concludes the one and begins the others. The final sentence of Chapter 27, "What happened to Sprog?" (a dwarfish character in *Akthelt and Gunnel*) anticipates the title of Chapter 28, which in its Austrian adventures is otherwise unrelated: "What Happened to the Hashish?" (Chapter 29 in turn is titled "What Happened to Sprog?" and is answered in less than four lines, before the action shifts to New York.) From the last line of Chapter 17 to the first of Chapter 18, the bridge is aural, the sound of a telephone ringing in Tulpen's New York apartment and then, in the next chapter, ringing more than a year before back in Iowa City. These words and sounds indicate a deeper thematic structure, of course, and show how Trumper's difficulties are uniform and persistent no matter where or when. Occasionally, these thematics form the link themselves, as when Chapter 15's concluding reference to Trumper's problems with his father (and how he has named his son for a more favored black-sheep uncle) introduces the next chapter, which is titled "Fathers & Sons (Two Kinds), Unwanted Daughters-in-Law & Fatherless Friends." The most traditional of Irving's linking devices are flashbacks, but even here the narrative conventions are stretched across such extraordinary gaps in time and space that the associations depend upon the author's deft use of all three persons of narration. When Irving shifts from Trumper's first person to the more objective third, the same events are seen in a different mood; and when there's an occasional use of second person, the effect is even more intimate. But these are first of all grammatical considerations, and any thematic implications which follow must first of all be established on the level of sentence structure.

The internal links are more subtle—perhaps even subliminal in their ability to make a seemingly random and disorganized book cohere, which is a lesson Irving learned from his teacher at the University of Iowa, Kurt Vonnegut, who was just then perfecting the same technique to help unify *Slaughterhouse-Five*. The points registered in this way are intentionally small, so that the reader won't be overtly distracted. But on the other hand, these odd references, when repeated many pages later in a completely different context, suggest that the novel is cohering on levels other than simply theme or action. For example, the language-lab student, Lydia Kindle, is impressed by Trumper's "big voice" (p. 51) on the tapes he's made for her; three chapters earlier (although a year later in the chronology), Ralph Packer hires Trumper as a sound man for this same quality expressed in the same words, his "nice big voice" (p. 27). Half a book apart, both Trumper and his father think of Biggie as a large ship; Biggie herself unconsciously compares her rival, Tulpen, to a character described earlier in *Akthelt and Gunnel*; and every time Trumper introduces his son to animal life, whether ducks at an Iowa City pond or an aquarium fish in Maine, the creature dies. Like the set-piece narratives, Trumper's life seems to be going great distances, in many directions at once, but never making any creditable progress. The same old words and sentences keep recurring along the novel's winding road.

How then does the novel conclude? Only by an exhaustion of every other geographical and temporal location until

Trumper can bring himself intact to Maine, where the story finally ends. The Vienna episode is effectively closed with the death of Merrill Overturf, but at the same time (and at the conclusion of his Austrian trip, when the CIA returns him to the States) Trumper must close the door on his New York experience with Tulpen—this happens as he finds her in an apparently compromising situation with the ever lecherous Ralph. Iowa City's business demands more work, but Trumper returns there alone to complete his dissertation in virtual monastic servitude. By the penultimate chapter, John Irving's protagonist has tied up enough loose ends so that the time becomes appropriate for him to read reviews of and see the movie Ralph has made of his life. Here he learns that Tulpen's presumed infidelity is part of art, not life—she and Ralph were simply filming a scene for the movie. At the same time, he discovers that Tulpen is pregnant with his child.

Throughout the novel's final third, film has emerged as the proper vehicle for expressing Fred Trumper's life. For one thing, its medium is a continuous present. And the way Ralph Packer directs, it has self-apparent form—being about Trumper's life and about itself at the same time, as the opening scene indicates:

With the bits from the voice-over still the only sound, Trumper and Tulpen are looking into a tangled mess of tape which has spun off a reel and is spilling into a great wormy pile on the floor. Trumper shuts something off: *clunk*. With this noise, the frame freezes to still. There continues to be no sync sound. Ralph's voice-over says, "Stop it, right there! Now the title—hold it right there . . . " Then the titles for *Fucking Up* appear over the frozen image. "Music," says Ralph's voice-over, and in turn they appear over the frozen image: Bogus Trumper, in stop-action, is stooping to attempt to untangle a mess of spilled tape. Tulpen is looking on. (P. 205)

Yet the film is art, not life, which for Trumper has a necessarily therapeutic effect: "To be in Ralph's movie required that he get out of the movie he was in now, didn't it?" (p. 234). Above all, it teaches him the need for a new text. Taking a bathroom break from the filming, Trumper finds a copy of *Vital Telegrams* at the same moment Ralph barges in, seeking another of his odd connections (the telephone is in the lavatory). "Jesus," Trumper thinks, "I should keep a diary" (p. 248). He has nothing but an opening sentence—"Her gynecologist recommended him to me"—but that line, which is again a matter of syntax, suggests its structure: "What a way to begin a diary! The question struck him: How is anything related to anything else? But he had to begin somewhere" (p. 250).

In time, Trumper learns to manipulate the movie as a communicative device, splitting from Ralph and Tulpen by filming a scene announcing his departure and editing it in at the proper sequence. When he limps back to the Christopher Street studio from his disastrous trip abroad, he notes that he's once more stepping into a life of art. But art is precisely what Trumper has been making of his life—a comic, slapstick style of aesthetic—and his ability to resolve matters more satisfactorily depends upon his ability to emerge as a better storyteller. This becomes his new role in relation to Colm, now that Couth has taken over the parenting, and in it he finds some success. "You should always tell stories, Trumper knew, in such a way that you make the audience feel good and wise, even a little ahead of you" (p. 324), but before this point his own long and winding road has been too unpredictable for even the most attentive reader, who must depend instead upon the links of syntax for the story to hold intact.

At home in Maine, Trumper finds his disorganized life has been step by step reduced to a single function: telling Colm a revised *Moby-Dick* story (with the whale, not Ahab, as hero) so convincing that the magnificent creature itself will appear. "Such a miracle, he knew, would have been as much a gift to himself as to Colm" (p. 330). The novel's final chapter, "The Old Friends Assemble for Throgsgafen Day," puts everything else in order: Trumper settled in with Tulpen and their new child, Biggie and Colm safe and secure with Couth, and even Ralph Packer content with his new girlfriend, Matjie. From this peaceful center, Moby Dick finally appears, and with him comes the first page of Trumper's novel: "Her gynecologist recommended him to me" (p. 361). What was first a diary (life) is now a true story (art), and with Trumper finally underway toward a resolution, the novel itself can conclude: "Mindful of his scars, his old harpoons and things, Bogus Trumper smiled cautiously at all the good flesh around him" (p. 365). Moby Dick has indeed appeared, as Trumper's insight into himself.

Each of John Irving's novels is characterized by experiments with structure. His first, *Setting Free the Bears* (New York: Random House, 1968), was tripartite in organization. The first third, which served as his M.F.A. thesis submitted to Kurt Vonnegut and the rest of the Writers Workshop Faculty (which that year included authors as diverse as Nelson Algren and José Donoso, Richard Yates and Robert Coover), is a conventional narrative set in Austria and organized around a series of adventures with the narrator's friend, Siggy, whose name gives Book I its title. Thirty-seven short chapters (totalling about one hundred pages) plot their travels across Central Europe on an ancient motorcycle, during the course of which they pick up an attractive young woman named Gallen and revive Siggy's old plan to free the animals from the Vienna Zoo; the section concludes with Siggy's death. Book II, by far the novel's longest, shifts modes to become "The Notebook," twenty-two entries made by Siggy as he observed the zoo's routine from early afternoon to the following dawn; interspersed are chapters from his autobiography as a child during Austria's violent decades as a republic and after the Anchluss; the interpolations, we later learn, are thanks to the narrator's editing of two separate documents. In Book III, "Setting Them Free," the narrator put Siggy's old plan into practice, with predictably disastrous results. The effect of this combination would be similar to dropping Merrill Overturf's diary into the center of an otherwise chronological *Water-Method Man*.

The 158-Pound Marriage is a more straightforward work, a narrator's confessional tale of the sexual liason he and his wife struck up with another couple. Far less innovative than his first two novels, *The 158-Pound Marriage* allowed Irving to imitate the form of John Hawkes' *The Blood Oranges*, which reflects the chronology not so much of external events as it does the narrator's evolving and maturing stance toward them. Its importance in the author's own development becomes evident in *The World According to Garp* (New York: Dutton, 1978) and *The Hotel New Hampshire* (New York: Dutton, 1981). *Garp* is Irving's venture into consistently third-person narration, and its subject is the making of a writer—*The World According to Garp* bears close resemblance to John Irving's world according to fiction, for much of the biography is familiar and the repetitious, talismanlike objects are here again in abundance. And although Garp always appears in the third person, there is still a mixture of textual modes, for we get to read his first story and a healthy chunk of his most famous novel (the latter set in distinctively different typeface). *The Hotel New Hampshire* shifts back to Irving's more common first-person narration but still varies its modes, thanks again to radical displacements of time and geography: there are three Hotel New Hampshires, with an interlude in Vienna standing between the two American versions.

Why so many internal texts and variations between them? Irving's answer is simple and is also the key to his strength as a writer: to underscore the difference between fiction and life without purging the former of the latter. Rather than subtract life, Irving adds it, in all of its contradictory varieties. A scene from *Garp* illustrates this method. Garp is telling his kids a story, then concludes it—with striking modifications—for his wife. The kids assume it is autobiographical, but Helen Garp, herself an English professor, knows that it is mostly made up. Yet even she demands a coherent model—that in her husband's imaginative creation of the tale there be a certain standard of internal truth. Seeing so many parts change confuses her. "Which of it is true," she asks, "and which of it is made up?" Garp plays it as a game with her, always giving the same answer, which we can apply to John Irving's own multifaceted texts: "Every part she believed was true; every part she didn't believe needed work" (p. 193).

II. The Essay as Lyric

The forces of freedom which are in literature depend . . . on the labor of displacement he brings to bear upon the language.

—R. B.

John Updike's America

A S A FULL-TIME PROFESSIONAL, John Updike
has been writing in America since 1954, the year he
graduated from Harvard and sold his first short story to *The
New Yorker* magazine. His quarter-century tenure as a literary
artist is remarkable not only for its artistic success, but for the
fact that such a vocation is still financially possible—in Updike's case, by virtue of a reliably supportive publisher and
ready magazine market. As fellow novelist Joseph Heller had
to remind students (*Paris Review* No. 60 [Winter 1974]) in the
prime of his commercial popularity, "even if every word a
writer writes is published, he will almost surely have to sup-
plement his income, usually by teaching, or perhaps by marrying money" (p. 128). John Updike is one of the very few
artistically important writers in America today who has not
been forced to rely on either of Heller's options. The business
of writing fiction is his very life.

Living and writing in America have formed the substance
of Updike's published work. The great majority of his novels
and short story collections take for their subjects the lives of

relatively average people: kids growing up in small towns with ambitions of moving to the big city, young married couples finding their first small apartments and jobs, maturing men and women enjoying relative affluence in the suburbs and (as the quarter century ripens) going through separation, divorce, and remarriage. For Updike, the scheme is vaguely autobiographical, and although to keep things mundane he almost always makes his protagonist's job something other than being a writer, the self-consciously artistic language of these fictions more than compensates for the businesslike action described. Harry "Rabbit" Angstrom of *Rabbit, Run* and *Rabbit Redux* is a typesetter, and most of the boys in Updike's stories who have hopes of becoming great artists grow up to find themselves commercial illustrators, animators, or photographers. But the language in which Updike characterizes their thoughts and behavior, and the way he arranges and rearranges their stories—all bespeak a self-conscious artistry. Their lives, it seems, are Updike's own life of fiction.

Best known as a regular *New Yorker* contributor, most highly honored for his novel *The Centaur* (National Book Award for Fiction at home, *Le prix de meilleur livre etranger* in France), and most popular with the reading public for his novels *Rabbit, Run* and *Couples,* Updike frequently reflects on his own work in ways that offer several clues to his method as a writer. His first novel, *The Poorhouse Fair* (1959), was written in 1957 as a visionary statement of American life as it might be two decades later; two subsequent editions (1964 and 1977) have contained new and revealing forewords by the author, reflecting how America's ongoing history has variously confirmed or contradicted his suspicions. *Rabbit, Run* (1960) had its sequel eleven years later in *Rabbit Redux* and formed a trilogy with *Rabbit Is Rich* (1981). A brief memoir, "The Dog-wood Tree: A Boyhood" (1962), was preserved in Updike's first collection of nonfiction, *Assorted Prose* (1965). And in 1969, the author thought back on what he hoped would be no less than the first half of his life in the long poem, *Midpoint.* Memoir and poem are rich with autobiographical correspondences, inviting readers to assemble an American middle-class saga from his eighteen books of fiction. But the best re-harvesting of this work has been done by Updike himself, in two paperback originals which reprint, rearrange, and rein-troduce short stories from his six previous hardcover collections and sheaf of uncollected work: *Olinger Stories* (New York: Vintage, 1964) and *Too Far To Go: The Maples Stories* (Green-wich, CT: Fawcett, 1979).

"Olinger" is the name Updike invents for the fictional town which vaguely corresponds to his birthplace, Shilling-ton, Pennsylvania, where he spent a self-admittedly sheltered boyhood in the 1930s and 1940s. Like William Faulkner's mythical Yoknapatawpha, Olinger's ecology, sociology, and demographics conform closely enough to the author's own home grounds to satisfy readers who demand a "real life story," yet allow sufficient latitude for the writer's essentially imaginative work. "The Maples," Richard and Joan, are a fictional couple Updike wrote about from 1955 through 1976. Their biographical match-ups with the Olinger stories and with the Updikes' own marriage (1953–76) are numer-ous, although Richard comes from a town just across the nearby West Virginia border (where Rabbit Angstrom, flee-ing a place very much like Olinger and its neighboring city, met a dead end in a murky lovers' lane). Even closer are the comparisons these Maples stories invite with Updike's treat-ment of American married life in his later novels, just as

Olinger serves as a background for most of the earlier ones. By Updike's own choice, *Olinger Stories* and *Too Far to Go* have become the center of his fictional and visionary world.

At the heart of these two books, in turn, stands Updike's most important and most characteristic story, "Pigeon Feathers." First published in *The New Yorker* for 19 August 1961, it gave its name to Updike's widely praised collection the next year. It was made the centerpiece of *Olinger Stories* (from which edition the following quotations come), and by reference to theme and technique, it provides the informing principle of nearly all the Maples stories gathered up in 1979. In "Pigeon Feathers," Updike creates David Kern, a fourteen-year-old protagonist with a boyhood somewhat like his own, whose family's ten-mile move from town out into the country causes things to be "upset, displaced, rearranged." In the Foreword to *Olinger Stories,* Updike remarks how "this strange distance, this less than total remove from my milieu, is for all I know the crucial detachment of my life" (p. ix). Physical separation is the boy's first problem; cut off from school friends, town life, and familiar surroundings, he finds himself isolated as never before. But Updike's story leads to stirrings of a deeper alienation. Rummaging through his mother's dusty college books, David chances upon H. G. Wells's *Outline of History* and reads that author's account of Jesus, of how "he had been an obscure political agitator, a kind of hobo, in a minor colony of the Roman Empire" (p. 21). The boy, though never a religious zealot, is at once distanced from the familiar emotional center of his life. Characteristically, Updike frames this loss in carefully shaped language: "It was as if a stone that for weeks and even years had been gathering weight in the web of David's nerve snapped them and plunged through the page and a hundred layers of papers underneath" (pp. 21–22). It is not the thoughts (in a conventionally religious sense) but rather the simple existence of such a book which, "if true, collapsed everything into a jumble of horror" (p. 22). Far more than a challenge of faith, Wells's book has prompted in David "an exact vision of death: a long hole in the ground, no wider than your body, down into which you are drawn while the white faces above recede." The threat is nothing less than "extinction," which Updike phrases in visionary terms: "a tide of clay had swept up to the stars; space was crushed into a mass" (p. 26).

Shaken loose from the familiar beliefs of his childhood, in themselves little more than comfortable habits, David reevaluates the texts of his life. Dictionaries, the Bible, sermons, and Sunday school instructions—all are catastrophically dismissed. "He hated everything about them but the promise they held out, a promise that in the most perverse way, as if the homeliest crone in the kingdom were given the Prince's hand, made every good and real thing, ball games and jokes and pert-breasted girls, possible" (p. 37). Like Harry Angstrom in *Rabbit, Run,* David cannot find adequate words to counter this vision—not from his mother, not from his minister, not from any of the conventional sources upon whom one is supposed to rely. All he has are "dread" and "fear," the key terms from Updike's reading of Kierkegaard. And so David, who is created in turn by Updike's language, fashions a new world of values from natural details: the subtle radiance of barnlight, the smell of old straw, the "ragged infinity" of the natural world in which even the feathers of pigeons, nuisance birds he slaughters at will, are marvels of creation. As David buries these birds he is "robed in this certainty: that the God who had lavished such craft upon these worthless birds would not destroy His whole Creation by refusing to let David live forever" (p. 50).

This consistent scheme of narrative repeats itself throughout the selection from *Olinger Stories.* A young, sensitive protagonist is by spatial displacement led into a reordering of personal judgment. Particular details have first prompted a longing for the universal ("above the particulars the immense tinted pity, the waste, of being at one little place instead of everywhere, at every time," p. 5). That longing ultimately leads to the question of physical death. But death's vision is countered by more details—not necessarily transcendent in Christian fashion, but celebrated nonetheless as transcriptions of a creator's art. By the volume's end, the narrative spokesman, now grown to resemble the real John Updike in the most personal of details, thinks of this celebratory technique as part of his own writer's art, of every little squib of life "all set sequentially down with the bald simplicity of intrinsic blessing, thousands and thousands of pages; ecstatically uneventful; divinely and defiantly dull" (p. 137).

The endings of both "Pigeon Feathers" and the fragment quoted above, "The Blessed Man of Boston," confirm Updike's moral stated in the volume's Foreword: *"We are rewarded unexpectedly"* (p. vii). Of course, David will not live forever, nor would any such maniacally unselective book be a useful work of art. But Updike is in full control of each self-conscious irony, for the boy's and the author's innocent intentions have successfully challenged death. A relish for detail helps, for as another fragment states, "we have no gestures adequate to answer the imperious gestures of nature" (p. 140); transitory as we are, we must improvise with what we have. By assembling a catalogue of existence, Updike locates what he calls the "thin point" of "piercing survival." "Details are the giant's fingers" (p. 153), these stories tell us. Or, as one of Updike's rare writer-narrator answers when asked the point of all he has written, "We in America need ceremonies" (p. 185).

We are rewarded unexpectedly. Fifteen years later, this moral and motto is transformed, in the pages of *Too Far To Go,* as "all blessings are mixed" (p. 10). Within those fifteen years of American life can be found the aftermath of President John F. Kennedy's "Camelot," the experiences of Vietnam and Watergate, and then another half-decade of change in world economics. The very first stories are brought back from the even earlier years of Eisenhower's presidency and Kennedy's thousand days; every one of the seventeen stories and fragments re-collected here is stamped by its evolving historical time. But once more, Updike's personal scheme of things and his own sense of language are the collection's true subjects. The three-stage narrative structure of the individual Olinger pieces (initial sensitivity/challenge by rearrangement/triumph over death) is reflected in many of the Maples stories, and the second volume is reassembled and chronologically arranged just like the first. The initial stories of *Too Far To Go* overlap in matters of character, theme, and biographical reference with the fragments near the end of *Olinger Stories* and with the little correspondences to Updike's own life (such as makes of cars, personal habits, and even home addresses). The volumes are indeed companions, and just as Updike told an interviewer in 1968 (the comments are reprinted in his *Picked-Up Pieces*, p. 498) that "if I had to give anybody one book of me it would be the Vintage [edition of] *Olinger Stories,*" so his similar creation of a new work from the Maples stories makes *Too Far To Go* a good clue to his manner and methods of more recent years.

A typical Maples story will, like an Olinger piece, begin with a reference to or demonstration of the protagonist's sensitivity. But with ripening age and a deteriorating marriage, there comes a change in attitude, for Richard Maple's aesthetic judgments are sometimes wasted on frivolous or farcical details: a supermarket cabbage, overwrought art, or tasteless racial parodies. The narrative scheme of sensitivity, challenge, and triumph becomes at times more heavily ironic, especially when the references to *Olinger Stories* are kept in mind. At the book's end when the Maples are in court for their no-fault divorce, the presiding judge is noted to have "a polished pink face" which "declared that he was altogether good, and would never die" (p. 255)—a sad diminishing of David Kern's illusion of triumph at the end of "Pigeon Feathers." At one point, Richard becomes a victim of his creative memory, letting his imagination sentimentally rewrite the history of his marriage and then sealing it with a kiss. Throughout *Too Far To Go,* details of American life are less sublimely celebratory and more sardonically diminished. The promise of a sheltered boyhood—of anyone's boyhood, Updike seems to say—is not fulfilled by an unlimited future of blessed moments. All blessings, our older American man of 1979 reports, are mixed.

If *Olinger Stories* explains much of what goes on in Updike's early novels, *Too Far To Go* helps one understand his major works which followed: *The Centaur* (1963) and his transitional novel, *Of the Farm* (1965). The fate of married men and women in America is of course central to his novel *Couples* (1968), but even *Rabbit Redux* (1971) and *A Month of Sundays* (1975) are more heavily dependent upon the subject of sexual relations than the sense of shelter (and more rarefied aesthetic longing) so integral to the earlier books. And with *Marry Me* (1976) and the closing stories of *Problems* (1979), Updike begins what may be the next saga in his fiction: remarriage. Yet the seeds of his full-grown interest in marriage and divorce predate even the first Olinger novel, *The Poorhouse Fair* (1959). The earliest of the Maples stories, "Snowing in Greenwich Village," appeared in *The New Yorker* on 21 January 1956, with the Maples (and the Updikes) not yet two years married; but already outside interests are in the air, as figured by the attractively threatening character named Rebecca. By the fourth story, "Twin Beds in Rome" (8 February 1964), Richard and Joan are already discussing separation; and even in the two stories in between, Updike's narrator is regretting that "once my ornate words wooed you" (p. 34). and acknowledging that "romance is, simply, the strange, the untried" (p. 54).

The strange and the untried are Updike's new variation on the rearrangement scheme of *Olinger Stories,* for which an eager and heightened sensuosity is the perfect tool. Joan Maple is challenged by a need to redefine her identity—"housewife" must be replaced by some more dignifying role and name for it—but Richard is the true slave of words. "Mistress," "nakedness," and the like haunt him, all the more so because his childhood's America has become "this nation of temporary arrangements" which nevertheless lacks institutions and even gestures to accommodate his plainly sensuous interest in any woman not his wife. Divorce is regretted and is in fact experienced as a death for him and for Joan because happy marriage is a myth his childhood taught him. His and Joan's gesturings as they vacillate between divorce and reconciliation are meaningfully pathetic, for as fraudulent as their relationship has become, it is the only thing they really have. "He saw through her words to what she was saying," a narrator sympathetic to Richard notes, "—that these lovers, however we love them, are not us, are not sacred as reality is sacred. We are reality. We have made children. We gave each other our young bodies. We promised to grow old together." Though the marriage crumbles, "her gestures would endure, cut into glass" (p. 231), an image which Updike's own respect for fine creation (reestablished by careful imagery earlier in this same story) leads the reader to accept as sincere.

The larger structure of *Too Far To Go* eclipses its obvious history and is formed instead by the patterns of Richard and Joan's language: words which alternately tear them apart and knit them together as they discuss their marriage. Once more, despite the sometimes contradictory hints of a larger plan for life, carefully noted details are the most one can have, and Updike is the master of those details. In 1960, Rabbit had worried that his existence amounted to no more than the tacky particulars of his shabby life and so tried to compensate by creating a world of superior aesthetics (harking back to the successful creative plan of his high school basketball career). In 1971 (the year of *Rabbit Redux*), one of Updike's stories, later transposed into the voice of Richard Maple, finds the narrator shuffling about the house his family has just vacated for another and feeling guilty "that we occupied it so thinly" (pp. 147), that although the 300-year-old colonial home has offered archaeological treasures from America's past, "of ourselves, a few plastic practice golfballs in the iris and a few dusty little Superballs beneath the radiators will be all for others to find" (p. 148). Like so many of the Olinger stories, this Maples episode ends with a moral: "All around us, we are outlasted" (p. 154). Natural details, elevating and enriching in the boyhoods of *Olinger Stories,* no longer do their job so rewardingly; by necessity, they have been replaced with the intimate details of a twenty-year marriage. These shared associations have bred a private language, and when the relationship ends, the language and composite details do not disappear. Remarriage is a new lease on creative life, but it is not a simple and entire rebirth as the inconclusive turmoils shown among the couples of *Marry Me* make clear. As the last story of *Problems* more confidently concludes, experiences from a previous marriage form a lost Atlantis of stored memories, a part of one's self, once shared, which is now submerged but still really there. And though harder to reach, they are no less persistent, no less valuable.

"Life goes on; stray strands are tucked back," Updike wrote in his "Introduction to the 1977 Edition" of his first novel, *The Poorhouse Fair.* He maintains this optimism despite his younger writer's pessimism that "all is flux; nothing lastingly matters" (p. xix). For John Updike, of contemporary America's writers probably the one most deeply read in theology and religion, the details of existence are the makings for a love-hate relationship with the world. Death and immortality have been the contrary poles of his writing career. But against the conventional wisdom of what he calls the death-oriented futurism in H. G. Wells's *The Time Machine* and George Orwell's *1984,* Updike declares his visionary faith in the creative powers of language—his characters', and his own. In the second of his Maples stories, a piece first published in 1960 during the high promise of a still-young Maples marriage, a narrator finds words in James Joyce's *Ulysses* to woo his wife: "Smackwarm. That was the crucial word. Smacked smackwarm on her smackable warm woman's thigh. Something like that. A splendid man, to feel that. Smackwarm woman's. Splendid also to feel the curious and potent, inexplicable and irrefutably magical life language leads within itself." (p. 30). Seventeen years later, a poetic voice which vaguely but in a deliberately suggestive way resembles Richard Maple's will dedicate a book titled *Tossing and Turning* (1977) to a woman soon to become his second wife:

> When first he saw. Alas!
> Full tup. Full throb.
> Warbling. Ah, lure! Alluring.
> Martha! Come!
> Clapclop. Clipclap. Clappyclap.
> —*Ulysses* (p. [vii])

Words have been the saga in John Updike's life of fiction. And the words of any day's creation, unlike their fleshy promise, are never eclipsed or effaced.

Grace Paley: The Sociology of Metafiction

MORE THAN ONE OF Grace Paley's stories feature a writer reflecting on her art, asking herself why she writes. Her narrator is often named "Faith," whose children are always named "Richard" and "Tonto" (short for Anthony), and whose mother and father play similar roles from story to story. In her second collection, *Enormous Changes at the Last Minute* (New York: Farrar, Straus & Giroux, 1974), everybody is just about a decade older than in her first, *The Little Disturbances of Man* (New York: Doubleday, 1959). "It was possible that I did owe something to my own family and the families of my friends," her narrator suspects. "That is, to tell their stories as simply as possible, in order, you might say, to save a few lives" (*EC,* p. 10). Such has been the traditionally moral role for the fictionist, which here becomes a metafictional concern. But for all her friendships and stylistic allegiances with innovators such as Donald Barthelme, Mark Mirsky, and others of this manner, Paley holds fast to several older, sociological concerns. For one, she is a woman writing; and secondly, of even more importance, she is an older woman, divorced and remarried, mothering two nearly-raised children while coping with the economic and social difficulties of life in a not-too-fancy neighborhood of New York City. Thirdly, she is a writer concerned with the viability of her occupation, particularly from the posture of the woman that she is. Hence for Grace Paley, metafiction—fiction which explores the conditions of its own making—is a peculiarly social matter, filled with the stuff of realism other metafictionists have discarded. For them, realistic conventions have been obstacles to or distractions from self-consciously artistic expression. Only Grace Paley finds them to be the materials of metafiction itself.

"A Conversation with My Father" is Paley's metafictional model and at the same time pledge of allegiance to the traditions of storytelling. First of all, the convention of character is made experimental by an interesting enhancement. "Everyone in this book is imagined into life except the father," Paley states in the book's opening disclaimer. "No matter what story he has to live in, he's my father, I. Goodside, M.D., artist, and storyteller." This unconventionally "real" character, whose existence in the story is due to the most innovative of techniques, then argues with his daughter that her fiction be more conventionally realistic. She resists a simple causal plot, "the absolute line between two points which I've always despised. Not for literary reasons, but because it takes all hope away. Everyone, real or invented, deserves the open destiny of life" (*EC,* p. 162). At her father's prompting, she tells and retells a story, fleshing out character and adding narrative detail. But in typical Paley fashion, the ending remains open. "I'm not going to leave her there in that house crying," she protests. "Jokes, jokes again," the father complains, but the daughter is proficient in the ways of metafiction and of the new style of life which has spawned it. "No,

Pa," she argues, "it could really happen that way, it's a funny world nowadays" (*EC,* p. 167). Rejecting his argument for tragedy as unrealistic, she practices her own storytelling art with a more experimental sense of realism—here as those conventions are debated with a superrealistically portrayed character.

It is part of Paley's devotion to the emotionally true to reject a conventional notion of tragedy as too facile for her art. As an occasional journalist, she voices the same fears, arguing in "Other People's Children" that the massive airlift of presumed "orphans" from Vietnam did more to flatter self-congratulatory notions of righteousness and pity than to help the lost children of the war (*Ms.,* September 1975). This, too is a function of her storyteller's role: to speak "with a historic sense" of "a slightly older person," as a young lover tells her (*EC,* p. 133); to struggle to know the people she writes about, as Paley told an interviewer; and most of all to create a sense of reality where otherwise none would exist, even if only by speaking the characters' names—"so those names can take thickness and strength and fall back into the world with their weight" ("Friends," *New Yorker,* 18 June 1979, pp. 34–35).

The conventions of personal exchange as detailed by a realistic narrator are the substance of Paley's fiction. Often there is little more than those exchanges—no traumatic action, few compelling themes, no pageantry larger than life. Paley's world is deliberately small, rejecting the flashy tragedies and their easy tears in favor of "the little disturbances of man." It is the view most common to her typical character, who "could see straight ahead over the thick hot rod of love to solitary age and lonesome death" (*EC,* p. 126). What does life offer? "Just when I most needed important conversation, a sniff of the man-wide world, that is, at least one brainy companion who could translate my friendly language into his tongue of undying carnal love," she begins, "I was forced to lounge in our neighborhood park surrounded by children" (*EC*, p. 77).

By making the most of these small offerings, Paley throws the conventions of narrative art into high relief. Her narrators speak with a peculiar sense of animation: "It is something like I am a crazy construction worker in conversation with cement," one of them admits (*EC*, p. 25). In another story, a drunk and enraged husband holds a pistol "and waved it before his eyes as though it could clear fogs and smogs" (*EC*, pp. 113–14). With so little apparent action to work with, Paley cannot simply let the sun set; instead, it must assume the graphic dimensions of a Saul Steinberg cartoon to become "a red ball falling hopelessly west, just missing the Hudson River, Jersey City, Chicago, the Great Plains, the Golden Gate—falling, falling" (*EC*, p. 121). To articulate the real is not just to describe it; Paley's motive is to create, to find a language which takes the most familiar affairs and gives them fictional (that is, imaginative) life. Of her own father's immigrant view of the American flag: "Under its protection and working like a horse, he'd read Dickens, gone to medical school, and shot like a surface-to-air missile right into the middle class" (*EC*, p. 122). Sometimes there is a novel thematic twist, as when a group of ghetto mothers propose that "one month of public-school attendance might become part of the private-school curriculum, as natural and progressive an experience as a visit to the boiler room in first grade" (*EC*, p. 90). But even these curious plot inventions are made securely within the familiar world of middle-aged, postmarried life. Very little distracts from the human exchanges of Grace Paley's stories and the conventions needed for their expression.

One of her earliest stories, "An Irrevocable Diameter," demonstrates what the unconventional use of realism can do to enhance the effect of a simple story. Much as the superrealist painters try all sorts of methods to distance themselves from their subject and so emphasize the abstraction of technique—painting upside down, projecting photographic slides on the canvas and then painting so close to the image that its larger composition cannot be realized until the full work is done—Paley chooses her words with exquisite care. Far more care, it seems, than their homely subject deserves, as "An Irrevocable Diameter" seems like nothing else but a story told too many times: of an older man shotgunned into a marriage with a reputably innocent girl. Where does it all happen? Hometown U.S.A., of course; but Paley reinvents it by calling it "a quiet little suburb hot with cars and zoned for parks." The girl? As we might imagine, but then more: "certainly cared for, cheeks scrubbed and eyebrows brushed, a lifetime's deposit of vitamins, the shiny daughter of cash in the bank" (LD, p. 105). Like a superrealistic painter drawn to the unbelievably slick surfaces of American commerce, Paley adds one shiny metaphor after the other, until the series hits us with the effect of Richard Estes's endlessly reflective surfaces or Robert Bechtle's ranks and files of polished cars. The narrator has an odd but in-the-end justified way of viewing things (like the superrealists painting upside down), such as the way he computes his age: "subtracting three years wasted in the Army as well as the first two years of my life, which I can't remember a damn thing about anyway" (LD, p. 107).

The story's action? We know too well the beginning, middle, and end, just as Estes's store fronts and Ralph Goings' parking lots are by themselves deadeningly familiar. Yet the superrealists paint the conventionally realistic in an experimental, deliberately abstract way, making the familiar seem suddenly new, making us see what's always been before us in a shockingly new way. Paley has only the tired conventions and even sleepier plot and theme at her disposal, but with it she works a small miracle. As her narrator concludes:

Living with Cindy has many pleasures. One acquires important knowledge in the dwelling place of another generation. First things first, she always has a kind word for the future. It is my opinion that she will be a marvelous woman in six or seven years. I wish her luck; by then we will be strangers. (*LD,* p. 123)

Grace Paley's journalism shows the same writing talents as her stories, reinforcing the sociological importance she has found within the metafictional motive. Her essay on the air-lift of Vietnamese children to the United States alternates statistics with personal asides, creating a rhythm which at once personalizes her research and lends authority to her passing observations. "The war in Vietnam, which began in ignorance, self-congratulation, and the slaughter of inno-cents," she notes in an assessment quite literary in scope, "ended in much the same way" (p. 69). But her statistics are equally effective, marshalled in a way that their effect is dev-astating. Would not all those Vietnamese "orphans" have suffered without our intervention? No way, Paley replies, and cites the fact that of 50,000 homeless children Nigeria re-fused to let out for adoption after the war in Biafra, all but twenty-seven were eventually reunited with their families or village communities within two years. She sees a self-serving drama in the parties at work, from the adoption agencies who feared losing their contracts through the self-promotion of World Airways (which used the airlift publicity to lobby for a domestic license) to President Ford himself who made the "cynical political decision . . . to use the children in order to dig military aid for Thieu out of Congress." As for the inten-tions of the American people themselves, surely humanitar-ian and disinterested as far as politics and financial gain, Paley again uses a literary technique, "the iron-hearted god of irony" who points out the subtle contradictions of handicapped, racially-mixed children of the Vietnam War being brought to a racially prejudiced country infamous for shunting away its own handicapped orphans and ill at ease with its Vietnam vets (p. 70). She even finds solid justification for expressing her feminist sensibility, an important fact in her short stories. "I must say that I don't believe women could have invented the insane idea of transporting these children," she confesses. "Most women were wild at the thought of the pain to those other mothers, the grief of the lost children. They felt it was a blow to *all* women, and to their natural political rights. It was a shock to see that world still functioning madly, the world in which the father, the husband, the man-owned state can make legal inventions and take the mother's child" (p. 96). The entire affair was a "kidnapping," which both as image and as rhetoric Paley can support only by calling upon her finest literary talents.

Yet neither is her metafiction an autobiography. Instead, life and art interact in Paley's work to the imaginative benefit of each. Compare her reminiscence, "My Mother" (*Ms.*, May 1980), with the story, "Mom" (*Esquire*, December 1975). In each, the vehicle of expression is less outright statement or even portrayal than it is the capture of a gesture: in fiction the mother figure leaning out a window, in life her mother standing in the doorway, in each case cautioning or caring for the child who now writes. Twice Grace Paley tells us "Then she died," but each time looking back again to another remembered gesture which in its characterization manages to live once more. Self-conscious attention to the devices of fiction thus serve the intelligence of life, which is metafiction's most fruitful sociology.

Robley Wilson's Experimental Realism

THAT THE CURRENT vogue in realistic fiction is something other than a reaction against the full-blown, anti-mimetic experimentation of the 1960s can be seen from a look at the four volumes of stories by Robley Wilson, Jr. His sixty-one pieces, appearing in a variety of magazines (from *Antaeus* to *Esquire*) over the past fifteen years, are all more conventionally finished than the innovative fictions winding up and down during these same years. We have, for example, none of Donald Barthleme's witty fragmentism, no evidence of Richard Brautigan's wild expanse of metaphor, and little of Robert Coover's self-conscious fabulation. Yet Wilson's work resists the "realism" label so appropriate to the stories by the masters against whom these experimentalists revolted: O'Hara, Cheever, Updike, & Co. Instead, Wilson has chosen to treat the short story's conventions—plot, character, theme, and a mimetically structured narrative—as experimental devices in themselves. Written in such full awareness of the aesthetic revolution in fiction, Wilson's experimental realism reinterprets traditional narrative art for our time.

The simplest of Wilson's stories reflect his own life: young manhood in Maine, Air Force duty in Occupied Germany, marriage, writing poetry, and teaching English in the Middle West. His apparent realism draws its color from a remarkably limited palette of cited experience: the shattered European landscape in the decade after World War II, the fragile emotional field shared by maturing husbands and wives, the agony of spirit of a poet who cannot write. In Wilson's fiction, these qualities pervade a life that is doggedly middle class; a favorite topic is the family cat—emotions for which can run the full range from love to anxiety and even terror, because so much contemporary history lurks in the shadows. At his most serious, Wilson writes of and for a generation gaining its maturity in the 1950s, inheriting a relatively colorless decade for its own and enervating it with the style and spirit that Auden would say created "the age of anxiety." As one of Wilson's poet-antagonists admits, "There's no immortality in the Twentieth Century—not even for the Immortals" (*The Pleasures of Manhood,* p. 126).

The subtle tension between man and wife is the most consistent theme in Wilson's early volumes, *The Pleasures of Manhood* (Urbana: University of Illinois Press, 1977) and *Living Alone* (Canton, NY: Fiction International, 1978). Sometimes a third party, a rival male, sparks the action, though a love triangle (as in simple realism) is never the point. Instead, as in "The Pleasures of Manhood," the issue is sexuality itself as an imaginative quality—the story's protagonist is most excited not by jealousy nor titillation but by the ridiculous adventure of helping an old friend give his wife a lavish barbershop-style shave, so that she might experience first-hand one of manhood's pleasures. What happens between a husband and wife is almost too complicated to measure and certainly too subtle to express in the soap opera of mannerist behavior. Hence, Wilson's stories feature a series of weirdly offbeat scenes: a crop-dusting husband thrilling his wife by buzzing their home, as he pleases himself by seeing her cut down in his machine-gun fire; another couple who parry their inheritances of cancer and insanity; and most remarkably a family who follows after the mysteriously receding tide of a disappearing ocean, only to be engulfed in its catastrophic return.

The horror of man's helpless vision—this description, from a story of a young poet's old instructor now gone mad with suspicion and hallucination, marks the outer limit of Wilson's fiction. For even in clinically realistic situations, the imagination is still the supreme agent of its own world. The imagination unleased, turned paranoiac and murderous, is just as much a threat as the same power atrophied. Each extreme destroys the human life around it, and through his range of dramatized situations Wilson shows how the imaginative faculty is indeed the soul of man, responsible for the tone and spirit of all else which happens in life.

In this respect, Wilson stands momentarily with his more self-consciously innovative colleagues. A few of his stories are honest examples of virtuoso writing; "Loving a Fat Girl: A Diary" is one such occasion. As a diary, it is an anti-illusionary form true to its own textuality; and its subject—loving a ridiculously obese, gigantically and repugnantly fat whale of a woman—is equally an excuse more for meditation than for action. Situations are devised for imagining the unimaginable: "I forced myself to look at her as I had not before," the protagonist writes, "and I slowly came to terms with her pig-like face, those features nearly submerged in a swell of cheeks and chins. I took in her bloated figure straining the seams of a tasteless print dress, her fat legs exerting great geometries of force against the threads of her stockings" (*LA,* pp. 63–64).

The story is a test for his writing, his writing a test for his imagination, his imagination a test for the original dare to the reader: "How may a man think of loving what he cannot endure?" (*LA*, p. 65).

In a more traditional vein, Wilson uses his talents for descriptive language to characterize events, set a tone, and establish a mood. Introducing the seascape which will be the setting for his story about the mysteriously receding and returning ocean, he notes the blandness of the region which invites his characters' disregard for the true danger at hand. "Rocks and split black ledges met the thrust of the sea with a kind of stubbornness, and brief reaches of lowland were strewn with coarse stones the ocean was rounding into its own toys," the narrator notes, but then adds in diminishing qualification: "At the tip of the Point was something fairly worth calling a cliff; at high tide it dropped off five or six feet to the water; at low tide it became nearly impressive" (*PM*, pp. 1–2). The water recedes to reveal a new landscape more like an ocean of the moon; but rather than dwelling on the awesomeness, Wilson has his characters quickly domesticate the wonder with picnic baskets, family jaunts, and half-baked plans for quaint adventure. But the ocean—the ocean we all know as a powerful and threatening force—is still there, and Wilson's deft manipulation of these traditional devices gives us something quite experimental: a story whose ending writes itself, as the ocean inevitably returns.

Fineness of detail is another aspect of traditional fictive art, crafted by such writers as Updike and Cheever into the deftly noted quality which tells all. It explodes into pure virtuosity and daring with Brautigan, whose experiments with metaphor put as much distance as possible between the factors of tenor and vehicle. Within this range, Wilson charts a middle course: his comparisons are tight yet telling, pertinent yet surprising in a way which saves countless words of exposition. "Good cheer," he begins his story, "Let Us Be True." "There is insanity in my wife's family, and cancer in my own," his narrator reveals. "We sit, the two of us, at the twilit ends of our respective days, and wait without talking about them for these twin legacies to come into our lives." But what does this waiting mean? A detailed simile tells all: "They will come like the postman on magazine mornings, cracking open the storm door with a startle of swelled wood, and they will slap down to the sills of our wedded senses, heavy and final and stumbled over" (*LA,* p. 9). The techniques of poetry—the unity of alliterative "s" sounds, a carefully extended controlling image, a word picture animated by a sense of narrative action—here serve the purposes of the most traditional fiction, but in a way which draws attention to their craftsmanship of technique. Once again, Wilson's realism is an experimental mode.

A favorite ploy is to take a madly improbable event and follow it out to a logical conclusion, using along the way all of the narrative devices more commonly associated with straight realism. In his text anthology, *Three Stances of Modern Fiction,* edited with Stephen Minot (Cambridge: Winthrop, 1972), Wilson describes this style as "premise fiction," which holds the middle ground between conventionally "mimetic fiction" (as written by Updike) and the more daring "dream fiction" favored by the experimentalists of the 1960s. Within this central category, Wilson includes his own story, "The Apple," which concocts one such premise. A neurotic young woman has projected an affair with a passive, utterly unresponsive mate: an apple. She dates the apple, love-talks it, cuddles it, quarrels, and suffers through an endless series of recriminations, as her life falls in pieces around her. It is all handled with clinical precision, even to the dark comedy of her confession when discovered at the story's end: "It isn't what you think" (*PM,* p. 69). Another less startling piece, "The Demonstration," contrives a more comically batty situation—old people from a rest home picketing a funeral parlor—for the sake of witticisms stenciled on their protest signs and the irony of their conversational exchanges with the mortician ("Is nothing sacred?" he complains). A more complicated story, "Addison," begins with another silly contrivance: an airman pretends his left arm is dysfunctional, but as his narrative progresses it crosses paths with other airmen handicapped in weirdly complementary ways (glass eyes, artificial legs) until the entire Air Force has reduced itself to absurdity, with the narrator's arm quite realistically amputated.

What makes these stories effective is the cool assurance of mimetic techniques applied in the service of outrageous improbability—never, Wilson is careful to establish, impossibility. "Not much is said these days about the girl gangs of the forties and fifties," one such story begins in deadpan, unassailable realism; of course not much is said about them, because there were none. But the trick has been played, and the narrative tone has itself already taken the reader that one necessary step into self-created plausibility, which the story sustains by its documentary tone and massing of wacky sociological detail. Two pages are sufficient to box the reader into an unlikely but inescapable conclusion, just what the writer wants him or her to think: "The girl gangs were not a threat to men, but an inspiration. We daydreamed, we fantasized, we desired, we were raised up" (*LA,* p. 88).

Wilson's best work displays his talent for orchestrating the narrative shape of short fiction. With his combination of unlikely subjects and the most familiar of narrative devices, he writes stories which display their own artifice without ever resorting to an anti-mimetic device. "Norma Jean Becoming Her Admirers" is one such piece, a fable about a mysterious visit from a deceased Marilyn Monroe which is realistic about its very ghostliness: "Help me, she says. She walks toward me, through me, into the room behind me. Help me" (*PM,* p. 82). From here a narrative develops in which the narrator is utterly absorbed into the heroine's mystique, until—at the story's fitting conclusion—he cannot refuse even her request for an overdose of sleeping pills. Fantasy meets reality with a truly immediate sense of closure.

"Saying Goodbye to the President," published in *Esquire* during the time of the Watergate scandal, is Wilson's most daring piece. Seven matching sections of narrative repeat different versions of one basic scene (at the time anticipated by most Americans): the narrator's personal farewell to a Nixon-like Chief Executive. Certain elements remain the same: similar beginnings ("We are strolling in the Rose Garden," "We are at Key Biscayne," "We are aboard the *Sequoia*"), recurrent details (such as the Secret Service lurking nearby), and repeated actions (centering on the President's last words). Each of the seven segments follows the same pattern: the President and the narrator are noted together at the point of farewell, comments are exchanged, condolences are offered, and the President departs—in increasingly peculiar ways. First, he merely goes back to the White House, then to a waiting van, next into the Potomac (in full scuba gear), and eventually to such absurdities as casting loose in a balloon, being bound and gagged in the trunk of a speeding car, and—at the story's end—being dismembered by a crowd at the airport. Because the particulars of each version differ, one is not compelled toward suspending disbelief; as readers, we

know that the entire situation is fabricated—all the more because its central character is a public person whose history is
known.

The key to Wilson's art is the manner of repetition within
repetition. Each time through, the story repeats itself in acci-
dental details, while the essentials grow in absurdity—from
the waiting van to the mob at the airport. What the reader is
most aware of is how the story is being told—repeated, as it
were, as an incremental fable. At no point is credulity self-
consciously violated; as with the tone in the "Girl Gangs"
stories, Wilson is forever assuming compliance with the details of his fully imagined world, and then sticking to his own
tone of realism by steadfastly using only realistic and mimetic
techniques. "Saying Goodbye to the President" manages to
be one of the most anti-traditional, experimental pieces of fiction to be published in a major magazine during the 1960s or
1970s, because its unique achievement is to accomplish all
the ends of self-conscious, anti-illusionistic art without ever
departing from the stock-in-trade of classic realism. By keeping to these familiar tools, Wilson has shown us what the stuff
of realism may really be about.

Looking back at Wilson's more somber (and less techni-
cally exciting) stories of frustrated spouses and lovers, we
find a familiar complaint: characters manipulate their own
lives not for any practical motives "but because it was another way of turning life into art" (LA, p. 24). Most of Wilson's people in such circumstances are artists; they have
failed in their creative work and so turn from lifeless can-
vasses and sterile pages to the more temptingly pliable material of their own lives. Here they are trapped. Life as lived
submits to the ultimately tyrannical realism, a historical necessity of socially shared imaginations which will not yield to
the individual artist's fancy. Such thematic awareness may be

what enriches Wilson's own flourishes with the realist's brush. When his characters are trapped in life, cut off from their art, they have little hope for imaginative freedom. When one of his narrators *is* in control, those very constrictions become the tools of liberation—for author as well as character.

Dancing for Men (Pittsburgh: University of Pittsburgh Press, 1983), which received the Drue Heinz Literature Prize the same year Wilson won a Guggenheim Fellowship and saw the magazine he edits, *The North American Review*, honored for the second time as America's most distinguished publication for short fiction, displays as a collection the same artistic control his protagonists seek. The volume's structure replicates the experience of reading Wilson's fiction in general, as the reader is first introduced to the social commerce of signs and then shown how even these materials are reducible to language. Wilson's signs are eminently human affairs: not shorthand references or escapes from the necessary business of fiction, but rather literary constructs which reveal the seat of reality itself, that conflux of human attitudes which create the life we live. For human beings privileged with rich imaginations, life is indeed a literary affair, as the experiences we construct take on the qualities of lives as fiction. There are lessons here, certainly for the moral conduct of human affairs, but first of all for the process of reading. Before we can interpret and judge our lives, we must know how to read the materials out of which they are made: experimental realism precedes any notion of moral fiction.

The signified objects of life can never be grasped, at least in terms of satisfying fiction; the thing-in-itself is the province of scientists and philosophers, not story writers. But the signifiers can be known, and known intimately well, for as the material product of our language they are the things we touch ourselves and offer in commerce with others. Wilson's stories in *Dancing for Men* are rich in circumstance, but always with situations which yield themselves to understanding in language—these are stories meant *to be read.* How else can one explain the husband's dilemma in "Despair," where the routines of workplace and home have become intolerable not in a concretely physical way but as a language statement: "How much trouble is it to make a casserole?" he asks his wife—not that the casserole as a thing-in-itself (a signified reality) matters, but because it is the legible sign of so much dissatisfaction in his life. "How hard is it to put something in the refrigerator for a hungry man who's worked hard all day trying to sell American cars to people who'd rather buy Jap?" (*DM,* p. 4) he demands, a patently unanswerable question which nevertheless speaks volumes. His wife is not reading their situation correctly, he means to say, and does. The title story, "Dancing for Men," is also an exercise in modes of reading, as a young woman dresses up as a boy to gain admittance to a carnival strip show and see the dancer's act. Again, the confrontation is less with the thing itself than with its sign, in this case the projection of a neon-light affair spelling out "MELITA." Deconstructionist criticism has taught us that women read differently than men by seeing through the structuring systems which determine how certain notions should be received. Dressed in male clothing, the woman becomes a subversive reader, gazing at the same ostensible thing-in-itself as her gentlemen counterparts in the audience but seeing an entirely different reality, since her interpretation of signs is a world (and sex) apart.

In "Thief," a self-styled urbane and attractive man is victimized by his own misreading: an attractive young woman takes advantage of his would-be wolfishness to steal his wallet and plant a stolen one on him; that the affair has been instructional is proven when several weeks later, after his proper humiliation, his wallet and money are returned. "Artists and Their Models" demonstrates how drawing and writing, as expressive extentions of the act of reading, invade the subject's private sense of identity: when something's drawn or written, to be seen or read, it becomes an object itself, made and added to the world—certainly something apart from its ostensible subject which justifiably feels robbed and misrepresented. Contrary signs abound in Wilson's third collection: the opposing masculine/feminine and father/mother readings of experience in "Crossings," the differing signals a woman reads from the behavior of her live-in lover and a visiting exterminator in "Wasps," and the way conventional signs of school-girlish romance are knocked askew by being acted out within an asylum for the insane. Any change in the observer's angle of vision, Wilson implies, creates a new reading experience, reminding us that the process is subjective rather than objective and that the world described is ultimately in our own minds. "Land Fishers," for example, finds a woman departing from her customary set of values and rules for behavior when her world is transformed—physically by a flood which makes her home an island and emotionally by the company of a young burglar out scavenging in these topsy-turvy circumstances.

The first two-thirds of *Dancing for Men* exploits this mode. Its stories become exemplary fables and cautionary tales, set right within our own social times, of how human intercourse is largely the manufacture and exchange of signs. All human problems, Wittgenstein suggested in the formulation which characterizes our transactional age, are principally problems in language. As an experimental realist, Wilson's role has been to highlight these problematics while all the time remaining solidly within the recognizable world of human action—for after all, Wittgenstein's theorem is reversible, that all problems in language are essentially human problems, which is something the more arcane practitioners of innovative fiction might neglect. The larger aspects of Wilson's control, therefore, can be seen in his ability to find the crux of fictional relationships in signs, for signs are humanly manageable even if what they represent is not. *Dancing for Men* concludes with a more specific application of this same technique: seeing how signs themselves are creatures of language. And it is for this concluding sense that the reader has been so carefully prepared.

With its five component stories (each running just three to six pages long), "An Inward Generation" is a testament to Wilson's narrative ear; it serves as the perfect complement to *Dancing for Men*'s concluding piece, the eleven-page story, "Paint," which demonstrates the fullness of the writer's art when all these peculiarities of words and signs are put into disarmingly natural play. "Meadow Green, 1939" captures a young boy's anguish at being unable to read the signs of sexual congress left behind by oblivious adults, while "War Games, 1952" concludes with the narrator reflecting back on some momentary M. P. duty as providing his "first clear, sharp insight into the several things that have to be understood about 'our boys' and the evenhandedness of war" (*DM,* p. 130)—by its use of quotation marks, another reading problem. Other stages in the narrator's life revolve about communication, from the fatuousness of a chain letter ("The Cause, 1962") to "Proposing, 1975," which is told entirely in dialogue. The most remarkable of these very short fictions is "Business, 1947," for here a young man's first job in the city provides not just a learning of the ropes but an introduction to the linguistic surfaces of a new world. The bearer of this new language is an older, veteran employee named Osborn, characterized by his phrases "That's the ticket," "There's a dandy," and "Let's go, scout" which guide the younger Jim Baxter through his routines of life and pace the ongoing cautionary monologue. These routines have the same gentle order as his verbal pattern, with little more substance: cafeteria food, a flophouse room, and a style of life with little beyond its trek to and from work. But to Osborn it's the big city as opposed to his idea of Jim's small town home. "This is freedom," he keeps telling the boy, "and that's the ticket for us" (*DM,* p. 124). Almost immediately, however, Jim bolts, fleeing the world Osborn would construct for him, since it *is* simply a world of language in which the word "freedom" bears relation only to Osborn's defensive justification of his own life's choices.

"Paint" is told in the present tense, happening before us like a movie. "She begins her weekend as usual" (*DM,* p. 143), we're told about the protagonist who remains unnamed despite the succeeding identifications of her husband, children, and friends. The first disruption is when she's caught a few dollars short at the supermarket: for this simple want, her previously unquestioned construct of grocery shopping is disruptively undone, forcing her to extract a few items from its syntax (peanut butter, bacon, three packages of frozen vegetables) and try to continue along. But her next step is even more maddeningly foiled, as her husband, who's been painting the front and back steps, will not let her in the house. His "You can't come in," based as it is on the factor of wet paint, is understandable, yet its effect is to ban her from her own home—or at least that's how she receives it. As with her shortage of money at the grocery store, a momentary loss of step in the semiotic process strands her by herself, cut off from dealing with the objects at hand, whether they be the groceries or back door steps. For the rest of this day, she is effectively alienated from all the familiar structures of her world and drifts alone through a foggy atmosphere of motel life. But the next morning her return is uneventful, the past closing behind her with the seamlessness of water now undisturbed. "I don't see what difference it makes," her husband chides her in the end. "You've got back in, haven't you?" (*DM,* p. 153).

The fiction Wilson has collected since *Dancing for Men,* which is at this writing in manuscript as *Weights & Measures,* attempts to capture a sense of what exists beyond language, to weave stories around the unsayable and that which is out of articulation's reach. In these stories, the sign-bearing relationships of such works as "Despair" and "Dancing for Men" yield to a more isolated sense of finitude: a young construction worker facing the blankness of Wyoming, a son confronted with the long-delayed death of his father, a back-country New Englander with shotgun in hand standing off an indefinite attack on his rude aesthetics. As opposed to the carefully mechanical configurations in the previous collection, *Weights & Measures* often ends its stories in an eerie openness: the fully unresolved sense of the construction worker's life, the son's suspicion that even in death his aged father has outlived him, and the Yankee farmer's posture of staring down the barrel of his shotgun at nothing at all, a virtual Minuteman statue posed in readiness against a vacant sky— just as the young worker has been pouring concrete missile silos for a Minuteman weapon neither he nor his fellow workers can logically or emotionally comprehend.

As is customary, Wilson begins *Weights & Measures* with a story which teaches his reader how to read the following works. "Nam" is concerned with a veteran home ten years after the war and still suffering what his father-in-law calls shellshock, but whose circumstance is more complex and disturbing. His wife had miscarried the very same day he killed his first enemy, and now he sits virtually paralyzed before a school playground watching the children who are not his, all these years refusing even to complete sexual intercourse with his wife. As narrator, his wife articulates for the reader the sense that cannot (and which Wilson prefers not) be put into words: "It is this suspended quality of his life—this stasis—I am more and more perplexed by as time passes," for it seems the two of them are "wasting away to nothing because time is swallowing us" (*WM*, p. 11). As in Wilson's succeeding pieces, the story soon takes over for itself as the couple remain in the car, now run out of gas, and "sit here listening to the sound metal makes cooling down; it will be like music" (p. 13), the only articulation for the sense of loss he feels and which she has come to share.

Weights & Measures continues with stories of a primitive backwoodsman whose newly finished porch is "an extension eight feet deep and fifteen wide of his personal vision of the world" (*WM*, p. 20) which, once violated, leads him to any number of rationalizations to defend it; and of the young man in "The Eventual Nuclear Destruction of Cheyenne, Wyoming," whose friends cannot articulate their place in the business of the arms race (for which they labor) beyond "I reckon it's going to kill all of us anyway, don't you?" (*WM*, p. 58). Although the thought is vacuous, the lives these people lead are real, in a very real part of the world despite its sense of existing "outside ordinary time and space" (*WM*, p. 49). Wilson's story forces itself to face this inarticulation, reminding us that for all of the linguistic problematics of *Dancing for Men,* there does exist a world beyond language which it is fiction's challenge to convey. At times, Wilson can capture this sense not in language but in its rhythms, as in this paragraph of observations centered on the musings of a lonely farm wife whose thoughts move out across what she physically and mentally surveys, only to return to her isolated self even closer than before:

And the mornings were not quite silent. The chorus of crickets was constant, there was almost always a solitary robin chirping in one of the ash trees; from the state highway a mile to the north she could hear the roar, hollow at this time of day, of trailer trucks. Somewhere she had read that in silence, absolute silence, you could hear a high-pitched sound that was your own nervous system, and a deep, boiling sound that was the circulation of your blood. Then the crickets might be her nerves, and the far-off trucks her blood. She didn't know about the robin; something of the spirit, perhaps, that the scientists always left out. (*WM*, P. 64)

"Praises," the volume's most ambitious story, finds the right words to talk around an unspeakable condition, of a painter who finds himself "a widower in his middle sixties, whose reputation was remarkable at a time when his abilities had turned mediocre—an artist without the tools of his art, determined to hide from a world in which he was not allowed to rest or recover himself" (*WM*, p. 93). The unspoken articulation comes when he meets his old and closest lover, still unavailable to him except for the briefest interlude during which she reveals the scars of a double mastectomy. How to express their situation, the epitome of loss? "You've made me young," he tells her, with full emotional honesty. "And you've made me whole," she replies, a circumlocution which expresses their fate: "A beautiful lie makes beautiful the thing lied about" (*WM*, p. 137).

Deaths and destructions haunt the stories of *Weights & Measures*—fittingly so, for they are the occasions of life for which we most commonly lack words. Some of Wilson's short fictions approach these occasions with oblique eloquence, as when at the funeral of an old friend a sculptor himself so aged that he can no longer hold his tools confesses in eulogy, "I have nothing left me but my inspiration. I am as dead, my friend, as you" (*WM,* p. 158). Yet in the following piece, Wilson can do as well with our other common response to the unspeakable—humor—as a wife undergoes the inconvenience of living several weeks with her husband before he admits that he's dead. Patently absurd? Of course. But as a metaphor for how difficult it is to reconcile oneself to the loss of a loved one, a perfectly admissable device. There's even room for humor, as during part of the conventional rigamarole of zombie-hood, which includes not casting a reflection in mirrors, the husband is vexed to find he can't see himself when shaving. Of course when he cuts himself, he doesn't bleed: Humor is its own perpetuation. We laugh, as at a joke after a funeral. For the true matter of death—of loss, and of bereavement—there's nothing to be said. In "Favorites," the device is more realistic, as a wife's last domestic act before her death in an auto accident has been to prepare her husband's favorite dessert. Though he clears the house of her personal effects and of other objects of memory, he eats the dessert, prolonging it over several days, dividing its remaining portion into halves and then halves of halves, until this Zenian paradox forces him to confront the inevitable by eating what's left. To realize his wife's death, he has improvised a convention and made himself an experimental realist, happy at least that in his manipulation of this device the actual business of his life is put back into orderly control.

III. The Essay as Meditation

Because it *stages* language instead of simply using it, literature feeds knowledge into the machine of infinite reflexivity. . . . in terms of a discourse which is no longer epistemological, but dramatic.

—R. B.

John Gardner's *Grendel*

G RADUATE SCHOOL in the sixties. New and expanding universities such as Southern Illinois and
Chico State-California, where, uninhibited by the presence
of world famous senior mediaevalists, a young Ph.D. like
John Gardner can teach *Beowulf*, Chaucer, and the Arthurian
legends to his heart's content.

Graduate faculties in the sixties. Zany and nervous,
pushed to the wall by pressures in the streets, they revitalize
the curriculum, responsibilities, thesis requirements. "Why
not write a thirteenth book of *Paradise Lost*?" they suggest.
"Another Canterbury tale? A few more sonnets for the Cy-
cle?" Criticize by imitation, and criticism itself is not
exempt: Frederick Crews publishes *The Pooh Perplex*, John
Seelye rewrites the true adventures of *Huck Finn*, a professor
at Johns Hopkins invents a writer and becomes a scholar of
his fictitious work. Borges is the spirit that moves us.

Creative writing booms. The University of Iowa Writers'
Workshop steals the action from the town's pinball games, a
remarkable coup. Writers who do everything but write hun-

ker over the fancy games their novels have become, bathed in the fluorescent glow of spurious technique. "Why not," they suggest, "write a novel where people are silent and animals talk?" "Why not," someone counters, "write a novel in which the lines of print slowly disappear?"

Write a novel whose typescript margins are perfectly justified, left and right. A novel which never uses the letter "e." A novel in which every seventeenth word is "balloon." Why not? This is experimental fiction at its logical extreme, because it is never actually written, just proposed. Premise fiction with just a premise.

A doctoral student in this department absorbs it all, then sallies forth on his roan Volvo to Chico and Carbondale, toward tenure and promotion.

This is the world which produces John Gardner's *Grendel* (New York: Knopf, 1971).

From God comes the standard. It is enacted by a hero and recorded by the poet. Such a theory of art can only emerge from the 1960s as a reaction to its presumed decadence. But the self-serving technique remains, the artist's legacy from his graduate school training. This is the world in which John Gardner's *Grendel* is produced.

Its reputation and saleability are a a side-show trick. "The Beowulf legend retold from the monster's point of view," the paperback cover tells us even before the title. Friends recommend it simply because of its remarkable shift in perspective, another Writers' Workshop trick, this time actually performed. Under the same influence when he taught there, Kurt Vonnegut planned to have the pages of *Slaughterhouse-Five* darken to impenetrability as they marched on toward the trauma of the firebombing, which would itself take place on a page of utter blackness; then as the book moved forward and the days advanced beyond February 13, 1945, the print would gradually become readable. Vonnegut, trained by the newspapers and family magazines, survived and outgrew these tricks. Gardner, the Iowa Ph.D., remained infatuated.

Recite the life history of a telephone pole, of a pebble, of a rock. Magicians with pens, the Writers of the Workshop are told they can do anything. But like hotdogging baseball players, they sometimes confuse infield practice with the game and fancy-catch themselves right out of the league. By actually writing *Grendel*, instead of leaving it for pinball conversation in the late drunken hours of after-reading parties, Gardner entertains this risk.

On a more serious level, he also courts danger. Myths, he argues, perform a God-like function, organizing our values and expressing our best hope for moral behavior. Myths need to be retold, because from generation to generation we forget them (unless they're memorized for doctoral comps). But what happens to a myth's morality when its structure is diametrically reversed, turned inside out, and given a completely new voice? Does the lesson change, is behavior modified? Does the myth itself take on inverted value for our perverted times?

The action is the same, but watching it as we do from the other side of the fence the characters change radically. The once-noble humans are now foolishly jabbering beasts, mere jackals of the plain observed by Hemingway's leopard who's scaled the icy heights. Conversely, the monster loses his alien qualities and becomes familiar—not human, but known to us through qualities we might never have thought existed. What chiefly interests us in fiction is characters in action, Gardner writes a decade later. For the first time in English literature, Grendel has come within our comprehension.

How is Grendel characterized? To give him a sense of superiority, he's made to fume and bluster at the world's stupidity—stupidity of men, of animals, even of the cosmos itself. To make him seem familiar, Gardner has him mug it up like a music hall clown ("I reel, smash trees. Disfigured son of lunatics. The big-boled oaks gaze down at me yellow with morning, beneath complexity. 'No offense,' I say, with a terrible, sycophantish smile, and tip an imaginary hat" [p. 7]). The same characterization is used for another presumed beast, the Fire Dragon. "A certain man will absurdly kill me," this latter creature foresees. "A terrible pity—loss of a remarkable form of life. Conservationists will howl" (p. 70). At times, on cue, Grendel will speak a cunning Old English—"earth-rimroamer," "wolf road"—and other times effuse in lyrical prose like a creative writing student, but the technique is effective only as technique. On the level of effective meaning, the action is reduced to situation comedy, as the once-mighty monsters prattle in the slang and topicality of 1971 America.

More effective is the subject of both monsters' rant: men's flaws, their ridiculous "pattern making" and "empire building" which invite destruction in both philosophical and material realms. All of this is framed by Grendel's unique perspective, the first real narrative we've had by a preternatural speaker. "They were small, these creatures," Grendel first tells us, "with dead-looking eyes and gray-white faces, and yet in some ways they were like us, except ridiculous and, at the same time, mysteriously irritating, like rats. Their movements were stiff and regular, as if figured by logic" (pp. 23–24).

But who is Grendel's "us"? Just himself and his mother. Unthinking and brutish, Grendel's dam is no audience, so the monster's narrative must be addressed to men, a contradiction that doesn't bother Gardner as it should. Dramatic monologues from Browning's day to the present have played themselves off the audience's presumed reaction. That's why they are dramatic, just as the center-stage soliloquy of Shakespeare's drama demands the convention of the audience to hear it. But in *Grendel* the audience is human, and Gardner never explains why the monster should be speaking to us. It is as if he knows he has no audience, that men—by their narrow imaginations—will never hear him, and that while Hrothgar's tawdry world is elevated to glorious mythology by the Shaper, Grendel will remain to us forever the obnoxious, thoughtless beast.

In truth, Grendel speaks to one man: John Gardner. Experienced in mediaeval lore and rampant with his own Shaper's imagination, Professor Gardner intuits the poetry in Grendel's life. As conceived, the novel is a very private affair, as most of the unwritten Iowa City experiments have been. As written, the book posits an audience of readers, a strategy which then makes Gardner Grendel's voice. The idea of the book works better in party-talk description, for in executing it Gardner tries to have it both ways. *Grendel* is the ultimate science fiction, for its only integrity is as a novel of ideas. Once unleashed into print, the book becomes self-contradictory and may be praised for something which is not really there (such as enthused readers turning the monster into a shaggy Holden Caulfield).

Yet the monster towers above men. They drink, rant, and fall off to sleep while Grendel snatches cows. They waste their energy and ravage their environment, while Grendel, a prototype Smokey the Bear, tries to tidy up after them (remember, only *you* can prevent Anglo-Saxon epics, another sentiment of the post-Promethean 1970s). "The sun spins mindlessly overhead, the shadows lengthen and shorten as if by plan" (p. 7), Grendel rants, knowing that any imposition of order asks for trouble. Random recurrences in nature "torment my wits toward meaningful patterns that do not exist" (p. 11), and if Grendel's wits are troubled, men's have been ruptured.

In his own thoughts, in dialogue with the Fire Dragon, and in audience with Hrothgar's priests, Grendel is the spokesman of orderly disorder. "I understood that the world was nothing: a mechanical chaos of casual, brute enmity on which we stupidly impose our hopes and fears. I understood that, finally and absolutely, I alone exist" (pp. 21–22). The Dragon adds a touch of Heisenberg, more 1970s prattle to extend Grendel's basic thought: "We . . . are apt to take modes of observable functioning in our own bodies as setting an absolute scale" (p. 66), a false tactic indeed which our own age has exposed.

Men, of course, resist Grendel's notion of chaos, and the book's real action is the monster's subtle sympathy for their acts. The Shaper, or court poet, arrives to elevate men's work by artfully woven construction, but his most enthralled listener is Grendel himself, "my mind aswim in ringing phrases, magnificent, golden, and all of them, incredibly, lies. . . . Thus I fled, ridiculous hairy creature torn apart by poetry" (pp. 43–44). Next, the Queen's beauty enchants him, and even though he's tempted to kill her and "teach them reality" (p. 110) he forebears, cynically and comically undermining the possibility of heroism itself. At the end, it is Beowulf's whispering—his fiction making—which weakens Grendel and invites defeat. It's just an accident, the monster protests, but fiction has done him in. "Poor Grendel's had an accident," he whispers back. "*So may you all*" (p. 174).

The myth has been inverted: the male, aggressive, linear Prometheus is replaced by the female, passive, modal Proteus—the Shaper yields before the adapter as the earth's resources give out. *Grendel* is a story of the 1970s.

The character has been redefined: oddly human, blundering, susceptible to the same draughts of poetry which spin our heads. He perishes because there must be difference: as his threat creates Hrothgar's people, so their enmity defines him, and he lives only in fighting to the death.

Such is the story Gardner reinvents as antimyth: "that beauty requires contrast, and that discord is fundamental to the creation of new intensities of feeling," as the old priest tells Grendel (p. 133). His novel has been a story of education, growth, and destruction by the very same principles which have given him life.

Such an exercise is just that: a procedure *Beowulf's* teacher might undertake himself to revitalize his teaching of the masterpiece. In earlier academic times, it might have emerged from a brilliant seminar's discussion, spurred on by the professor's teasing questions. What if, the American modernist suggests, F. Scott Fitzgerald were to sit in on this afternoon's class on *Gatsby*? What if, the Miltonists ask, Satan had won? Or has he? John Gardner's *Grendel* takes us to these lengths.

Thomas McGuane: The Novel of Manners Radicalized

A TEA BISCUIT CRUMBLES, and in its fragments Henry James can read the fortunes of a social world. "Her voice sounded like money," Nick Carraway says of Daisy Buchanan, and in that manneristic notation we sense the compelling illusion of Gatsby's life. There's even a touch of it in Faulkner: young Thomas Sutpen is turned away by a servant at the rich man's door and forever vows to build himself an equal domain. Despite our relative incivility and egalitarian beliefs, who says there is no novel of manners in America?

But then come the American 1960s. On both social and artistic fronts, the old hierarchies crumble. Down with the establishment, and death to the novel. The politics of Berkeley, Madison, Columbia, and the 1968 Democratic Convention find their match in the communal rites of Woodstock and the anti-illusionistic fiction of Brautigan and Vonnegut. Apparent anarchy dislodges the old truths. The novelist's study of society now takes place in a madhouse, and the decade's most reliable narrator is Ken Kesey's Chief Broom, who in *One*

Flew Over the Cuckoo's Nest warns us, "It's still hard for me to have a clear mind thinking on it. But it's the truth even if it didn't happen."

Yet in Chief Broom's words can be found a clue to the new American novel of manners. *Why* is his narrative the truth, even though it may not have happened? Look back a few lines, as he characterizes his experience in Kesey's asylum. "I been silent so long now it's gonna roar out of me like flood-waters and you think the guy telling this is ranting and raving my *God. . . .*" The truth is in the telling, and for every step within the careful structure of janitors-orderlies-practical nurses-RNs on up to The Big Nurse herself, the Chief has a perfect image. Their manners are, in terms of this novel, a matter of his transforming language, finely tuned to each.

Kesey's novel helped signal a decade's revolution, and there are many writers who follow his example and in some cases even his lifestyle in the previously unwriterly northwest corner of the United States. Richard Brautigan, for example. Jim Harrison. Guys who know their way around a trout stream or high range better than through the pubs of Greenwich Village or midtown bars near their editors.

How this all translates into a new novel of manners, however, falls to Thomas McGuane. In his twenties during the 1960s, McGuane wrote his first published novel in 1968, that year of social and political turmoil which Michael Herr (in *Dispatches*) described as "so hot that I think it shorted out the whole decade, what followed was mutation." Through the next dozen years, as presidential candidates were assassinated, rock stars OD'ed, and the culture at large underwent a transformation whose sudden thoroughness was unknown in previous American history, McGuane produced four more novels plus a book of essays, while paying off his Montana ranch with oddball Western filmscripts for *Rancho Deluxe, The Missouri Breaks*, and *Tom Horn*. His fiction includes the full cast of counterculture characters, from dropouts to heavy dopers and theatrical rock stars. These protagonists both form and are formed by their cultural milieu, of which McGuane is a sharp observer. But it is in their language that they become true agents of fiction, factors in the new American novel of manners.

Although his first novel, *The Sporting Club* (New York: Simon & Schuster, 1969), is almost biblical in its microcosmic annals of a rich men's hunting and fishing lodge, McGuane's sharpest attention to manners comes with his introduction of young protagonists out searching for America and themselves. Nicholas Payne from *The Bushwacked Piano* (New York: Simon and Schuster, 1971), Thomas Skelton of *Ninety-Two in the Shade* (New York: Farrar, Straus & Giroux, 1973), and Chet Pomeroy who narrates *Panama* (New York: Farrar, Straus & Giroux, 1978) catalogue the manners of McGuane's three residencies since childhood: Michigan, Montana, and the Florida Keys. Payne has an ear for people's speech; a girl who thumbs a ride on his motorcycle out West complains, "I'll take a car any day. . . . You cain't play the radio own this" (p. 55). Skelton, heavy into drugs, hallucinates while hitching with a silent-majority-type salesman who can nevertheless find common ground and share perceptions: "When Skelton told the hardware salesman that the paint had just lifted off the whole car in a single piece, the hardware salesman agreed with him about how Detroit put things together. This was the epoch of uneasy alliances" (p. 5). But most impressive is McGuane's ability to convey the characteristics of his culture within the words and syntax of his narrator's own speech. Listen to Chet Pomeroy, the burned-out rock star, explain why he owns a pistol:

Something about our republic makes us go armed. I myself am happier having a piece within reach, knowing if some goblin jumps into the path, it's away with him. Here in Key West, we take our guns to parties. My pedal steel player had one on a clip underneath his instrument: it said "Death to Traitors" on the backstrap and was stolen by a fan in Muscle Shoals, Alabama, on New Year's Day. (P. 32)

This paragraph makes its point entirely by its conflux of manneristic references within the verbal rhythm of our era's popular idiom. Before it is a gun, it's "a piece." Adversaries are not individualized beyond a spooky presence, nor are they shot at or killed—they're just swept away by the cadence of the sentence. From here, the notations turn to rock culture: not just any music, but that from a steel guitar. And not just anywhere, but in Muscle Shoals, home of a major recording studio famous for the Southern Blues sound, and stomping grounds of the Allman Brothers Band, two of whose members died on motorcycles. Chet's way of narrating helps define the time in which he writes. *Panama* is the new American novel of manners.

Florida. "Drugs, alligators, macadam, the sea, sticky sex, laughter, and sudden death" (p. 28)—these are the elements out of which Chet constructs his novel. In his essays collected in *An Outside Chance* (New York: Farrar, Straus & Giroux, 1980), McGuane explains his own fascination with what another of his protagonists calls "America's Land's End." Both essayist and novelist must be sensitive to the little elements of atmosphere which typify a place, such as "the ground swell of

Latinate noise—that first of all things that make Key West another country." The town is "both an outrageous honky-tonk and a momento of another century," and even its biosphere is such that one gets the sense of living on another planet, where at a drive-in movie "the column of light from the projectionist's booth is feverish with tropical insects" blurring the image on its way to the screen, and when "driving home, palmetto bugs and land crabs pop under the tires" (pp. 79–80). That's from McGuane's essay on tarpon hunting for *Sports Illustrated*. For his fictional protagonists, Key West is a springboard to history and prophecy, but all based in the country's manners which have their toe hold in this extreme piece of land. As Nicholas Payne observes,

He was happy to be in Key West. It was Harry Truman's favorite town and Harry Truman was fine by Payne. He liked Truman's remark about getting out of the kitchen if you couldn't stand the heat. Payne thought that beat anything in Kierkegaard. He also liked Truman's Kansas City suits and essential Calvinized watch-fob insousiance of the pre-Italian racketeer. He enjoyed the whole sense of the First Lady going bald while the daughter wheedled her way onto the Ed Sullivan show to drown the studio audience in an operatic mudbath of her own devising. (P. 169)

In just over one hundred words—quickly enough to leave undisturbed his narrative's progress through Payne's business in south Florida—McGuane evokes thirty years of American popular history. Double-breasted suits, the President's snappish wit, long-suffering Bess, daughter Margaret on Sunday night TV: such is the Americana of Payne's childhood which he rediscovers in such cultural time pockets as the Keys.

Florida yields an apocryphal vision as well. Chet notes that a clip-joint parking lot is dug up to reveal the grave of an ancient Calusa seagoing Indian, who for decades has been "staring up through four inches of blacktop at the whores, junkies, and Southern lawyers" (pp. 6–7). In *Ninety-Two in the Shade*, Thomas Skelton takes his skiff out during a solar eclipse, glancing upward to see hundreds of birds circling a black hole in the sky, the same vacuity he finds in human relations. Times are bad. "Nobody knows, from sea to shining sea," this novel begins, "why we are having all this trouble with our republic," but McGuane's protagonists are determined to find out why. Their investigations take them to the heart of "hotcakes land," where the streets are lined with "franchized outrages" and "everything is for sale." But they can also locate themselves comfortably within an ambience constructed from the counterculture and uniquely local elements, as the author explains for Skelton:

Intelligent morning: Indian River orange juice, thousand-times-washed Levi's, perfect Cuban guayabera shirt, Eric Clapton on the radio, sunlight swimming the walls, cucarachas running a four-forty in the breadbox, mockingbirds doing an infinitely delicate imitation of mockingbirds. Yes, gentlemen, there is next to nothing; but I'm going to have fun anyway. (P. 76)

Skelton's trick is to "look askance and it all shines on" (p. 155). His two closest studies are the fishing guides Faron Carter and Nichol Dance. Carter is the less distinguished, known best for his pink wedding cake of a wife Jeannie, a former baton-twirler whose titillating half-time act has been a monument to "a whole civilization up shit creek in a cement canoe without a dream of a paddle" (p. 138). Dance is more original, at home in Key West as America's terminal man who has fled a murder rap up North to see his car, smoking from a jammed brake drum, ignite and explode on the town's main street—"Nothing to do but stand back and watch her go" (p. 8).

Skelton measures the distance between these two guides and their methods, computing an average of manners for the Key. But in the end, he favors Dance's extreme and becomes himself America's terminal man, burned out by the 1960s and murdered off Barracuda Key.

Nicholas Payne of *The Bushwacked Piano* is a more comprehensive hero, touching base with all three of McGuane's favorite regions. For him, Michigan is a place to escape: upper-middle-class parents who would suck him into the "Waring blender" of their homogenized lives, future in-laws who'd keep him out of their family unless he finishes law school, a rival boyfriend who's a perfect dud of a junior GM exec but who can dress like a department store mannequin, and so forth.

When Payne takes off, it is *to experience* things: a paragraph in which he drives his motorcycle along the California coast matches image-for-image a description McGuane included in his *Sports Illustrated* essay on riding the Matchless 500. His girlfriend and her family have taken off for their Montana vacation home; crossing its entryway, Payne feels compelled to mimic Ernest Hemingway's shotgun suicide. But as always McGuane has a sharp eye for manners and is an artist at summing up a character, even when with the girlfriend Ann Fitzgerald it's making the decision simply to inventory her room:

Protractors, lenses, field guides, United States Geodetic Survey topographical maps, cores of half-eaten apples, every photograph of Dorothea Lange's ever reproduced, tennis shorts, panties, a killing jar, a mounting board, fatuous novel, a book about theosophy, a bust of Ouspensky, a wad of cheap Piranesi prints, her diplomas and brassieres, her antique mousetraps, her dexamyl and librium tablets, her G-string, firecrackers, bocci balls and flagons, her Finnish wooden toothbrush, her Vitabath, her target pistol, parasol, moccasins, Pucci scarves, headstone rubbings, buffalo horns, elastic bandages, mushroom keys, sanitary napkins, monogram die for stationery, Elmer Fudd mask, exploding cigars, Skira art books, the stuffed burrowing owl, the stuffed, rough-legged hawk, the stuffed tanager, the stuffed penguin, the stuffed chicken, the plastic pomegranate, the plaster rattlesnake ashtray, the pictures of Payne sailing, shooting, drinking, laughing, reading comics, the pictures of George smiling gently in a barrera seat at the Valencia Plaza de Toros, an annotated *Story of O*, the series of telephoto shots of her mother and father duking it out beside the old barge canal in Washington, D.C., Payne's prep school varsity jacket, an English saddle, a lid of Panama Green, Charlie Chaplin's unsuccessful autobiography, dolls, a poster from the movie *Purple Noon*, a menu from the Gallatoire restaurant, one from the Columbia in Tampa, one from Joe's Stone Crab in Miami and one from Joe Muer's in Detroit, and one rolled skin from a reticulated python curled around the base of a stainless steel orbiting lamp from Sweden—in short, a lot of stuff lay wall to wall in a vast mess, upon which she threw herself with energy born of her separation from Nicholas Payne. (Pp. 101–2)

Why is this important? Not for *tour de force* writing, though it takes that talent to get the job done. Structurally there's the narrative need for an explanation—why won't Ann simply move in with Payne?—which that laborious inventory now makes clear. "Ann didn't want to pair off," we're told. "She wanted to play in her room with all that junk for a few more years" (p. 110).

Sharp-eyed and sharp-eared Nicholas adapts to Montana, jawboning it with a backcountry mechanic and studying the rodeo riders' techniques until he's figured out how to stay on a bronc for fifty seconds, winning Ann's esteem. But there's still more of America that he needs to immerse himself in before a true sense of himself can be found. Therefore it's on the road—less of a Kerouac tradition than an homage to Huck Finn, whose shore-bound troubles become things of the past once he's back in flow with the river. Highway A1A to Key West, a river of concrete which like Huck's Mississippi takes you to the extreme terminus before it all vanishes into nothing.

McGuane's facility with manners is evident once more in his ability to use them for parody. *The Bushwacked Piano*'s narrative follows parallel paths as Payne celebrates these cultural idiosyncracies while Ann mocks them. She writes poetry, shoots arty photographs, and reads D. H. Lawrence seeking to be "at one" with things; with Payne as her guide, she finds the best chances for identification in the "simple national archetypes like floozies, bowlers, and rotarians" (p. 146). In *Ninety-Two in the Shade*, McGuane himself is partial to such caricatured types, notably Faron Carter's baton-twirler wife: "Twirling, dropping to one knee for the catches, then prancing downfield in a mindlessness now growing culturally impossible, she was a simple pink cake with a slot" (p. 138). Jeannie Carter is a natural at this, but the effect is heightened when Ann adopts it as a role. As with McGuane's protagonists, her motives are fiendish: "In an epoch in which it was silly to be a druid or red Indian, there was a certain zero-hour solace in being something large enough to attract contempt." And so Ann looks forward to being a floozy "as another girl might have anticipated her freshman year at Vassar. With almost Germanic intentness, she had set her sights on being cheap and available and not in the least fussy." Pulling out the peroxide, hair spray, and heavy make-up, she faces the mirror. "Call me Sherri," she squeaks (p. 146).

Other elements of satire abound. The American entrepreneur is caricatured in C. J. Clovis, who sells multi-storied bat towers for ridding areas of their mosquito problems. The folks on Mente Chica Key who buy one are in turn satirized as the typical country bumpkins eager to be chiseled by this gentle grafter from up North. Proof of the parody is that none of these cameo shots is held in focus for long. Clovis vanishes like the fly-by-night he is, the gulled townsfolk fade away into the sunset of their gumbo manners, while Ann picks up and leaves Nicholas Payne for the finer styles of her GM junior executive, pausing only to stop at Neiman-Marcus first for a quick change back from floozy-hood. George meets her at the Detroit airport, she in an Oscar de la Renta ensemble complemented with sandals by Dior, he in jacket by J. Press, Pucci cravat, and seamless cordovans from Church of London. "See them" the narrative section concludes, "running thus toward one another, perfect monads of nullity" (p. 218).

With *Panama*, McGuane comes to the point where he can trust his protagonist with the narration. Chet Pomeroy is a rock performer, adept at theatricalizing his culture's dark desires, "paid to sum up civilization or to act it out in a glimmer" (p. 35). On stage he's done this with his music; in *Panama* the effect is verbal, where Chet is no less a singer of his country's songs. Sometimes the quotations are direct, as when he's mourning the loss of his girlfriend and acknowledges that he's got heartaches by the million, or listening to another girl explain that "bad luck and trouble is getting to be my middle name" (p. 41). If I didn't have bad luck, I wouldn't have no luck at all, and happiness is a thing named Joe. *Watch the words*, his girlfriend cautions him, and Chet appreciates how "the occupational hazard of making a spectacle of yourself, over the long haul, is that at some point you buy a ticket too" (p. 52). In terms of manners, Chet has become a communal catalyst, having "poured blood from my head so that strangers could form a circle" (p. 43).

In the tropical atmosphere and shabby economics of Key West, Chet finds it easy to be the poet of decay. Everything's for sale and nothing's worth buying. What good there's been is swept away by dubious progress, reminding Chet of the manners of his time: "Today an old family jewelry store had become a moped rental drop; a small bookstore was a taco stand; and where Hart Crane and Stephen Crane had momentarily coexisted on a mildewed shelf was now an electric griddle warming a stack of pre-fab tortillas" (p. 165). Nature itself seems ready to rebel, and the air reeks decadence. Chet's narrative eye is on present manners and their long-term consequence, a vision both timely and millenial—here, with its lyric language, is another key to the new American novel of manners. "When they build a shopping center over an old salt marsh," Chet approvingly observes, "the seabirds sometimes circle the same place for a year or more, coming back to check daily, to see if there isn't some little chance those department stores and pharmacies and cinemas won't go as quickly as they'd come" (p. 8).

Self-consciously the artist, and so ingratiated in the reader's mind, Chet can introduce lines of poetic imagery without disrupting his ongoing sense of story. Offbeat characters can be introduced with a savor for their individuality, and examples of extreme behavior blend easily with Chet's manner of storytelling. Take Marcelline, his girlfriend's girlfriend, distinguished by her scandalous habits and kinky sexuality. She robs graves, blackmails sugar daddy lovers, and is as ready to jump into bed with Chet's girlfriend as with him. A perfect counterculture extra who herself doubts she's a survivor: "I might be gone in the next reel" (p. 42). How does the new American novelist sum this all up? In the perfectly concise sentence capped with a image unique to Marcelline's innocently charming idiosyncracy, as "a leggy, otherwordly beauty, trailing her dubious dreams and pastel whoredom like a pretty kite" (p. 49).

Above all, Thomas McGuane is a novelist of manners because of his ability to single out the characteristics of an age and to know his characters through them. Coupled with his narrative ability to blend these details into a convincing pitch, such aptness of notation helps create the spirit of the times and of his protagonists. Listen to Chet complain, with a style and vision which give us a feeling of his woes:

For some reason, scarcely anything seems to bespeak my era so much as herpes simplex. Oddly, it appears as—what?—a teensy blister. Then a sore, not much, goes away, a little irritant. It's infectious. When your girl gets it, from you, it is not at all the same thing. For instance, she screams when she pisses. She won't put out. She demands to know, "Where did you get this one?" The answer is: *From the age.* (P. 81)

From the cultural conflux, Chet has drawn inward to the most intimate physical details and then suddenly reached outwards again, just when his girlfriend asks for a specific explanation. The specific is explained by the general *when each is closely realized*; in his ability to modulate the two within a convincing narrative, McGuane becomes the surprising heir to Fitzgerald and James.

Richard Yates: The Power of Sadness

IT IS WRITTEN on his face.

Look at the dust-jacket photos on each of his books from 1961 through 1981: the late-developing *naif* shown in the first, who looks a decade younger than his thirty-four years, will within the next twenty age two lifetimes.

Give Richard Yates that old photo from *Revolutionary Road* now and he'll growl, "What a wimp!" Ravaged by his work, he is proud of its testament to life's hard mortality. Fitzgerald partied, Hemingway excelled at sport, both living out a public version of their fiction. For Yates, it is simpler and more devastatingly powerful: he has lived within his work as well as around it, and that compulsion has generated both an *oeuvre* and an image that speaks to its power. Sadness is its own discipline.

Look back to Flaubert, James, or Fitzgerald, and you'll find a powerful union of language with incident, theme with technique. For the novel of manners to work effectively, this is how it must be. If "Madame Bovary is me" succeeds, it's because the author has made the little social notations of personhood a dominant technical factor in his work's construction, in his novel's very spirit. Those notations form the story, and the most compelling among them—when handled successfully—will generate the text which follows. For Richard Yates, it is the power of sadness which makes his work possible.

The titles of his two short story collections define the thematic center of each: *Eleven Kinds of Loneliness* (Boston: Little, Brown & Co./Atlantic Monthly Press, 1962) and *Liars in Love* (New York: Delacorte Press/Seymour Lawrence, 1981). And that thematic center is not what each story's about; it's what each story *is*. Not just what happens in the life portrayed, but what evolves within each story's formal structure—all this depends upon the generative power of loneliness or romantic disingenuousness. These issues possess the story as they have the man who wrote them. *Madam Bovary, c'est moi.*

In *Eleven Kinds of Loneliness*, the structure of sadness replicates itself. Each story's rhythm moves from a build-up of expectations to their inevitable letdown, a progress so inexorable that no contrary interest is allowed to intercede. Occasionally sadness prevails because contrary intentions miscarry, as in "Doctor Jack-o'-lantern" where a grade-school teacher's care for an alienated transfer student undoes his momentary triumph near the end, and as in "The Best of Everything" where the camaraderie of a bridegroom's stag-party friends actually serves to isolate him from the romantic interlude with his fiancee he's always desired. "Jody Rolled the Bones" shows how a transformation is aborted by a change of drill sergeants just as the initially reluctant men have come to learn and to like "soldiering," while "No Pain Whatsoever" follows a wife through the routine paces of a visit to her husband in the TB ward, the little details of his hospital life filling the narrative and holding back its inevitable conclusion until the very end when the story's painfully evident tone and structure collapse completely and the wife surrenders to her solitary tears.

Sometimes the reverse happens, with the lonely climax telegraphed to us at the very beginning. "The B.A.R. Man" begins with an explanation of its conclusion: "Until he got his name on the police blotter, and in the papers, nobody ever thought much about John Fallon" (p. 129). Then Yates immediately gets down to business, supplying all the little details about John's work and home life which indeed show why nobody would think about him very much at all. These stifling details in turn generate some narrative movement: John flees an unwanted Friday night engagement with his vapid wife and winds up in a bar where he encounters some better prospects with two younger Army men heading for a night club. Yet John is still not the type of guy to be bothered over; the girl he's matched with resists his line, and returning to their table with fresh beer he finds the group has ditched him. The story begins its second-last page before John's evening comes to something, but that "something" is as fully anonymous as he is. Noticing a group protesting a left wing rally, John suddenly attacks the harmless, undefended speaker. What on earth is happening?, the reader asks—until we remember Yates' opening line. Now the effect of John's isolation is complete, for even making the police blotter and newspaper has been a totally pointless affair.

Sadness nurtures itself: when something indefinite is made definite, nothing becomes any better, and what are developed as phoney little mannerisms soon consume their actor. Yates takes painstaking care with the shabby affectations of a would-be journalist who apes a columnist's habit of wearing a battered waterproof hat:

He developed a whole new set of mannerisms to go with the hat: cocking it back with a flip of the index finger as he settled down to make his morning phone calls ("This is Leon Sobel, of *The Labor Leader* . . ."), tugging it smartly forward as he left the office on a reporting assignment, twirling it onto a peg when he came back to write his story. At the end of the day, when he'd dropped the last of his copy into Finney's wire basket, he would shape the hat into a careless slant over one eyebrow, swing the overcoat around his shoulders and stride out with a loose salute of farewell, and I used to picture studying his reflection in the black subway windows all the way home to the Bronx. (P. 104)

What would otherwise be a paragraph of static description becomes a kaleidoscope of active verbs—cocking, tugging, twirling, shape, swing, stride—each generated by the first manneristic affectation of the hat.

Once generated, these manneristic conventions take on a life of their own, impelling Sobel through the ludicrousness of his own pilot column and his eventual dismissal from newspaper work. The strength of these illusions is shown at the story's end, when the narrator's well-meant phone call with another job lead is haughtily rejected by this sad character who's convinced he's a major writer.

Yates can do just as well with stasis. Walter Henderson is introduced as a nine-year-old whose favorite game is "falling dead." His romanticized attitudes of collapse eclipse their frame of war games and cops and robbers to become an activity by themselves. Twenty-five years later finds him essentially the same person, relishing his inevitable sacking from a job he really can't afford to lose—"a chronic, compulsive failure, a strange little boy in love with the attitudes of collapse" (p.

79). When he decides not to tell his wife until he has secretly found a new job, that too runs movies in his mind, perfect complements to her own "carefully studied effects" and the "orderly rotation of many careful moods" that are her life (p. 90). When his plan fails and she demands the truth, he has the perfect response:

"Well, darling—" he began. His right hand came up and touched the middle button of his shirt, as if to unfasten it, and then with a great deflating sigh he collapsed backward into the chair, one foot sliding out on the carpet and the other curled beneath him. It was the most graceful thing he had done all day. "They got me," he said. (P. 93)

The most effective tales of sad loneliness, however, are those which rhythmically open and close according to the same inevitability, like breathing in and breathing out. "A Really Good Jazz Piano" celebrates a hopeless loser whose one claim to success dissipates before his eyes, leaving him worse off than before. At the tale's caesural center, Yates announces the change of fortunes with that most natural of references, "Everything went wrong the next day" (p. 159). Ain't it the truth? So it goes. These are the structures of Yates' best stories. The unthinkable and therefore immediately rejected notion of companionship, which begins "Out with the Old," another TB ward story, is in the end embraced, after a disillusioning trip home for a failure of a Christmas holiday. The saddest thing of all about loneliness, Yates can show, is its inexorable return.

And what do we have in Richard Yates' stories when we don't have loneliness? Ghostly presences, as he calls them at one point. A character turns back from a window through which he's been staring, "leaving a shriveling ghost of his breath on the glass" (p. 185). When the employer fires Henderson, he lifts his hands from the glass desktop, leaving "two gray, perfect prints on the glass, like the hands of a skeleton"; the sacked employee stares at them, "fascinated, while they shriveled and disappeared" (pp. 80–81).

In *Liars in Love*, the more closely thematic situation of falseness between lovers again provides a structural order and the energy to generate a narrative. Sometimes the disingenuousness is deliberate and direct, as the false friendship between two divorced women finds its reflection in the way their respective children subtly bait each other. Other times it is more convoluted, as a daughter's claim to her father that she no longer loves him is formulaically repeated, twenty pages and many years later, to the husband she's about to leave. At best it is a subtle *leitmotif* which, when it comes to dominate a story, signals the resolution far better than would any neat typing up of plots. After the neatly ordered children's world of "Oh, Joseph, I'm So Tired" is dismantled by one character's dishonesty and another's hysterical overreaction to it, the narrator thinks back to the trick his sister taught him of listening at bedtime to the city's sounds, the part of his experience he remembers best. Even in her youth she is able to lyricize it, and it is the poetry which remains with her young brother:

"I don't just mean the loud noises," she said, "like the siren going by just now, or those car doors slamming, or all the laughing and shouting down the street; that's just close-up stuff. I'm talking about something else. Because you see there are millions and millions of people in New York—more people than you can possibly imagine, ever—and most of them are doing something that makes a sound. Maybe talking, or playing the radio, maybe closing doors, maybe putting their forks down on their plates if they're having dinner, or dropping their shoes if they're going to bed—and because there are so many of them, all those little sounds add up and come together in a kind of hum. But it's so faint—so very, very faint—that you can't hear it unless you listen very carefully for a long time." (Pp. 18–19)

Like the paragraph generated by Leon Sobel's hat, these lines build on from the young girl's enumerative imagination to form a sense the boy holds dear. Several times later, as his mother's witless activity complicates the story, listening for the city's hum as he falls asleep serves as a satisfying coda to the day. But as is inevitable in Yates, all that's built up must come down, most finally the sound of the city which the youngster has never been able to hear, even as the story ends:

There would be no more school in our room. We would probably never see Bart again—or if we ever did, he would probably not want to see us. But our mother was ours; we were hers, and we lived with that knowledge as we lay listening for the faint, faint sound of millions. (P. 33)

———————————

The expansion and contraction of Richard Yates' work, built as it is around the human mortality that sadness and loneliness convey, is signalled by the smallest and subtlest of elements: a character's affected mannerism, a *leitmotif*, a child's cheap music box whose "dim, rude little melody it made suggested all the loss and loneliness in the world" (p. 99).

This toy becomes the central object of "Liars in Love." The protagonist's three-year-old daughter has forgotten it in London, after she and her mother have left him for home. Unable to make legitimate friendships, he picks up a prostitute at random, but in bed, "in wholly unexpected grace and nourishment, she became a real girl for him" (p. 105). The assignation expands into an affair, and the affair could grow into a real love were it not for his better pleasure in the whole image of the thing: "Memories of Christine in his arms whispering 'Oh, I love you' made him smile like a fool in the sunshine, and at other moments he found a different, subtler pleasure in considering all the pathetic things about her—the humorless ignorance, the cheap, drooping underwear, the drunken crying" (p. 114). But when she casually and jokingly places an image on him—of a man who lives off a prostitute's earnings—he revolts, and the love soon collapses. He leaves her—and at the end, as he packs for his return to America and a reconciliation with his wife, forbids her even a phone call. Sweeping out his room, he comes across the music box once more, which is now charged with deeper meaning. He plays it "slowly, as if to remind himself forever of its dim and melancholy song. He allowed it to call up a vision of Christine in his arms whispering 'Oh, I love you,' because he would want to remember that too, and then he let it fall into the trash" (p. 139).

Flip back now through Richard Yates' dust-jacket portraits and see a man reborn. The hunched-over vision of someone so worn by writing yields in just the three years back from 1981 to 1978 to a picture of resurgence, of Walt Whitman-like jauntiness to his eyes, shoulders, and smile—a look perfected and refined from the more hollow-looking photo of 1976. But ah, 1975! A flash of *savoir faire*, with beard and hair just fashionably greying and neatly trimmed above the smart military shirt, eyebrows arched in a confidently skeptical look directly at the camera. Then back to 1969, a clean-shaven 1962, and finally that 1961 shot of a man far too young and innocent to have written *Eleven Kinds of Loneliness*, even though its final story had been finished that year. Books can be flipped through backwards, and it's in these books that Richard Yates prevails.

IV. The Essay as Witness

"Writing makes knowledge festive."—R.B.

Betrayed by Jerzy Kosinski

[*Note to the reader*: You are reading what is known as a *samizdat*—an informal essay prepared for circulation among friends and editors in circumstances where formal publication would seem impractical (the term originates with Soviet dissidents who were denied easy access to the established media.) I first wrote it in February 1981, drawing on partial drafts dating back to October 1979 when I returned from a brief visit to Poland where I had lectured on contemporary American fiction for the Ministry of Higher Education. Its purpose was, and still is, to set the record straight on the two Kosinski pieces that I'd done much earlier for the academic press: "Jerzy Kosinski: An Interview" (conducted in November 1971, first printed in the premier issue of Joe David Bellamy's *fiction international* [Fall 1973], and then reprinted in Bellamy's anthology *The New Fiction: Interviews with Innovative American Writers* [1974]) and the chapter on Kosinski in my study *Literary Disruptions: The Making of a Post-Contemporary American Fiction* [1975]. Even before going to Poland, I'd begun to note inconsistencies among the autobiographical stories that Kosinski had told me, and by the summer of 1979— when I'd read galleys of his forthcoming novel, *Passion Play*, and heard conflicting reports bouncing around New York—I came to regret having endorsed his unverifiable material as scholarly fact. Kosinski's autobiography seemed to have been reinvented for a transient market at each turn of events.

At the same time, I began to dislike his newer fiction, which disappointed me with its self-indulgence and gratuitous cruelty—two familiar charges which his earlier novels had successfully withstood. Therefore, when the Chicago *Sun-Times* asked me to review *Passion Play*, I submitted a notice praising some of its good elements but deploring its "anti-democratic fascination with the very rich." When the review appeared on September 2, I sent a copy to Kosinski, adding that I felt badly about this new direction in his work. "Even 'Stupid Ludmilla,' " I told him, referring to a tormented character in *The Painted Bird*, "was loved," whereas *Passion Play* was disproportionately hateful and overwrought. A few weeks later, Kosinski phoned, wishing me a good trip to Poland and saying that he didn't mind the review, even though it had "followed him around the country"—apparently the Field News Service had put it on their wire and local papers covering Kosinski's promotional tour had reprinted the piece nearly everywhere he appeared. Abroad, I heard even more conflicting stories about Kosinski—not rumors but points of fact, such as those concerning the political circumstances in the Soviet Union and in Poland at the time that he had left. Because of the conflicting stories that Jerzy himself had been telling me, I felt obliged to sort out my own experiences with the man and his writing.

Happily, I can report that, for good reasons, his texts survive intact. For the very same reason, however, his autobiography does not. Since I first drafted and circulated my *samizdat*, there have been a great number of essays published in its wake, most notably Barbara Gelb's "Being Jerzy Kosinski" in the *New York Times Magazine* (21 February 1982), Geoffrey Stokes and Eliot Fremont-Smith's "Jerzy Kosinski's Tainted Words" in the *Village Voice* (22 June 1982), and John Corry's "A Case History: 17 Years of Ideological Attack on a Cultural Target" in the *New York Times* "Arts & Leisure" section (7 November 1982). All were front-page stories.

I still consider myself a critical advocate of Kosinski's literary work, and I admire his skill and charm as a self-publicist (talents to which I myself succumbed). The "betrayed" in my title is an allusion to Manuel Puig's novel, *Betrayed by Rita Hayworth*, in which the act of betrayal is gently seductive and pleasurable even in retrospect—yet a betrayal just the same.]

IT WAS JERZY KOSINSKI on the phone—an instrument which he uses like a whip—and his shrill voice was snapping out instructions with an intensity which gave everything he said an aura of truth and authority.

Everything. Before, it had been such matters as his traumatic childhood in war-torn Poland (context for *The Painted Bird*), the pranks that he'd enjoyed playing on Soviet and Polish officialdom before his surreptitious flight to the U.S. (*Steps*), his claims against the collectivizing force of the American news and entertainment media, especially TV (*Being There*), and a whole series of adventures, object lessons, and caustic lectures about life in the modern world (which are pretty much the topics of *The Devil Tree*, *Cockpit*, and *Blind Date*, the other novels which he'd published up to then; a few years later, I'd be able to recognize his own climb to national and world celebrity-hood in *Passion Play* and *Pinball*). As they would appear, Kosinski would embellish the stuff of these novels with frantic conversations about his own life, whether on television talk shows, in formal interviews for magazines, popular and academic alike, or in the sudden and disturbing phone calls that one was liable to receive virtually anytime, day or night.

The drama, it now seems, was a product of method acting. One had the sense—and maybe Kosinski believed it himself—that he was calling from a bus station phone booth, rushing you the most crucial important news as his bus was starting to pull away.

And here was Kosinski again, creating a verbal structure within which I was to read the galleys of his new novel, *Passion Play*, which, he said, he'd mailed to me that morning.

"It's about a *polo player?*" I asked with some surprise. His last two books had favored characters closer to Kosinski's ideal of himself—Tarden the master secret agent, Levanter the speculative investor—each of them disposed to travel the world giving demonstrations on how to live securely and how to practice sweet revenge. So why this suddenly new interest in polo?

"Don't you know?" Kosinski, now in a more subtle mood, invited me to ponder. "I have been a semi-professional polo player for the past seven years. In fact, I've just come back from a tournament in Dallas. Next month we'll be playing in Oak Brook, near Chicago—that's close to you, so why don't you come see?"

I didn't make it to Chicago, nor did I have to. *People* magazine later showed me and a million other Americans a six-page photospread of Kosinski at his hobby: dressing like a polo champ, in action on the field, and faking shots from a sawhorse installed on his Manhattan apartment balcony. Seven years of polo playing! How could I have missed all this?

Passion Play itself, filled with information about the sport and packed with allusions to his own work as well, read with typical Kosinski authority. Fabian, the polo-pro protagonist, was a writer, too, and his books on horsemanship stood in perfect parallel with the titles and contexts of Kosinski's own novels: from *The Runaway* (trauma from early accidents), through *Obstacles* (a warning to unseasoned riders), and up to Fabian's latest, a *Blind Date* look-alike called *Prone to Fall*. *Obstacles*, Fabian's equivalent to the National Book Award novel *Steps*, had even won the "National Horse Lovers Award." Like Kosinski at Yale, Fabian occasionally taught a university seminar, here called "Riding Through Life." The parallels were endless, and topping them all was Kosinski's proficiency in polo, the point at which his and Fabian's lives touched most intimately. Seven years of polo playing! I'd obviously overlooked a substantial chapter of his widely publicized in-progress autobiography.

The novel was still several weeks from publication when I visited New York to interview another writer. We finished our work, and in the small talk which took us to the door, the subject of Kosinski's work came up.

"Are you seeing anybody else while you're in town?" my friend asked. He knew that an afternoon of shuttling up and down the 7th Avenue local would take me to the doorsteps of several other writers that I'd been working on, from Donald Barthelme in the West Village to Jerzy Kosinski up on 57th Street.

"No," I replied. "Barthelme's down in Houston, and Kosinski is off somewhere playing in a polo tournament."

"Polo?" he laughed.

"Of course," I proudly announced. "Kosinski has been a semi-pro polo player for over seven years!"

Now my host was really chortling. "Why, I taught Jerzy how to ride last summer in Central Park!" he announced.

Inventing his own life of fiction is Jerzy Kosinski's most natural act. His novels record this process, and virtually everything he does reinforces his writing and further secures his own existence. The process becomes involuted, the fabrication of circles within circles: who was Jerzy fooling, the critic who was led to believe that there had been a seven-year career in polo or the writer who supposed that he was teaching him to ride? In Kosinski's world, each act is equally suspect. Like a secret, the real Jerzy Kosinski remains unknowable, inviolable, secure.

He has made this a program for his fiction, and he is fond of quoting Proust: what our memory recalls is just as arbitrary, just as creative, as any act of the imagination.

Our memories are neither more nor less authentic than dreams. Fair enough. But when your childhood is filled with horrors from the war and with memories of unspeakable atrocities practiced on a very personal level—atrocities which you survived simply by your own cunning—the imagination's role becomes creative indeed.

As a six-year-old child, Kosinski was stripped of all the structures and buffers of civilization and quite literally tossed to the wolves of superstition, hatred, and despair. *The Painted Bird* is the fictional event distilled from this past, from memories themselves at least partly fictional. The Boy in this novel is a survivor, as they say, because he too can create—and in not very pretty ways. As Kosinski admits in his comments on the novel:

Maybe hate is a way of self-fulfillment? For hate takes on a mystical aura; to possess hate is to possess great power, and the wielder of that power has control of magnificent gifts. Like Prospero he rules his kingdom, and justice is meted out according to his will. Things are as he sees them to be; if not, they soon submit to his vision of the world. He can shape his world as he wills: Prospero's wand becomes revenge. (*Notes of the Author*, p. 27)

Masters of revenge are indeed the protagonists of each Kosinski novel from *Pinball* back to *The Painted Bird*. Creative revenge, not destruction—that's what makes these books readable, even enjoyable and, most of all, instructive.

The problem is that Jerzy Kosinski's life of fiction goes on night and day, on and off the page, influencing lives other than his own. Stories about him rebound as reactions to the sometimes cock-and-bull narratives that he's created about himself or perhaps to rumors whose seeds he has planted to spice up the plot. Does he work for the CIA? This is a common rumor, sparked by his continual jet-set travels. Does he, as he once told me, donate all of his novel royalties to a charity account for orphans like himself? Does he really believe that the figures and even the print runs of his books "cannot be revealed" because "the Arabs" would use it for publicity against his cause? He has no visible means of support, but a reasonable supposition is that he might simply have invested the earnings from his two pseudonymous books on collective behavior, *The Future Is Ours, Comrade* (1960) and *No Third Path* (1962): each was published by a major commercial house—Doubleday—and one was both serialized in the *Saturday Evening Post* and condensed by *Reader's Digest*.

Questions about Kosinski's life, lately front-page matter for the *Village Voice* and the *New York Times* "Arts & Leisure" section, have been knocking around for years. There was talk of a young woman who was introducing herself around Manhattan (and being so believed) as the ghost-writer of Kosinski's novels; on widely separate occasions, Mike Krasny and Ron Sukenick told me about her without revealing her name. His written English was atrocious, the woman was apparently claiming; he merely sketched out the plots and she wrote them up. The truth of this accusation and others may never be settled, but Kosinski does play interminable games with his assistants, editors, and publishers: as his manuscripts go through copy-editing, he will, for example, purposely introduce silly little errors to keep in-house readers on their toes and to monitor for careless proofing. Like F. Scott Fitzgerald, he seems to regard typeset galleys and even page proofs simply as succeeding drafts, and he rewrites heavily at each stage. My own interview with him typed up as nearly one hundred pages, and after three exchanges of the manuscript, hardly one word remained the same. Jerzy has been known to take a paragraph out onto the street and quiz passers-by for their sense of its rhetoric—he did this for a passage in my *Literary Disruptions* which he didn't like. His apartment is lined with dictionaries, and few visitors can pass an hour in his presence without being plumbed for their sense of words. He's curious as to how native speakers of other languages might differently express a common event (having been raised in Polish and Russian, he worries about being linguistically conditioned by Slavic structures when writing in those tongues). In a deconstructive age which has exposed the prison house of language, Kosinski is a liberator par excellence.

As a matter of fact, his novels have tempted others to experiment and pull practical jokes of their own. A few years ago, California writer Chuck Ross typed several clean copies of Kosinski's National Book Award winner *Steps* and submitted them to major U.S. publishers—including Kosinski's—as original work. Predictably, it was not recognized; indeed, it was unanimously rejected as unpublishable.

It's the *real* stories, however, that are more troublesome: the ones which Kosinski tells about himself and which, while they have great pertinence in both form and substance for his fiction, are later contradicted by undeniable fact—often by a subsequent story that Kosinski himself tells a reliable journalist or academic scholar.

Sometimes, of course, Kosinski's flair for publicity is amusing and harmless. My first contact with him, for example, was back in the fall of 1971; he was one of many contemporary writers that I was just beginning to read and enjoy while teaching Hawthorne, Melville, & Company at Northern Illinois University. I sent routine requests for interviews; most authors would answer by letter, and some didn't answer at all. Only from Kosinski did I get the whole public relations treatment, as if I had written a tourist bureau for a bit of information and called down an avalanche of booklets and brochures on every conceivable attraction. I received *Notes of the Author* (New York: Scientia-Factum, 1963) and *The Art of the Self* (New York: Scientia-Factum, 1968), his self-published pamphlets on *The Painted Bird* and *Steps* (actually an English version of an afterword that he'd written for the German-language Swiss edition of the former and some self-advertisements for the latter which were published in the *New York Times Book Review*); there was even a copy of *Tijd van leven— tijd van kunst* ("the time of life, the time of art"), a Dutch version (Amsterdam: Uitgeverij de Bezige Bij, 1970) of the same two booklets with, as my colleague Gus Van Cromphout pointed out to me, extensive additions to the text packed with further clues to Kosinski's method of writing. Plus any number of photocopied interviews, essays, and remarks. If I'd been writing a doctoral thesis on the man, my research would have been half-done.

A meeting was arranged for several weeks later at Yale, where Kosinski was now teaching. Meanwhile, I worked up the material for my interview questions: the three novels to date plus his studies of life under Soviet collectivism and also the details of his personal experiences which had been appearing in print—his years as an abandoned child in wartime Poland; the odd jobs, some with underworld associations, that he'd worked during his first years in the States; and, most interesting (to me), his friendship and close artistic affinity with the film director Roman Polanski, whom he'd known since college days in Łodz. In the most famous story then circulating, Kosinski was described as being on his way to a party at the Polanski-Sharon Tate residence and missing it only because his luggage was misplaced en route. As everyone now knows, that was the night that Charles Manson's crowd showed up instead. So when our campus film series announced a Halloween-night screening of Polanski's *Repulsion*, I put aside my aversion for horror films and, since Kosinski's critical autobiography was obviously involved, made plans to attend.

Which was my first mistake. *Repulsion* is more than a horror film: it is a brilliant, if at times sadistic, exercise in the conditioning of an audience, to the point that even a subtle shift in light or break in the music sends unsophisticated viewers into shudders and screams (this was DeKalb, Illinois, after all). The mayhem and violence, and even the murders, are the least of it, for Polanski's worst threats (on which he delivers) are the ones that he makes to the irrational fears and unimaginable horrors that he himself cultivates within the audience's own emotions. Were there tonal similarities to *The Painted Bird*, published the same year? That was one good question that I wanted to explore. But here I was, screaming my head off through a damn fool movie! And I was to meet this director's long-time friend and artistic soul-brother in just a few weeks—what was I getting into? I should have stuck with Hawthorne and the nineteenth century, I told myself; those ghosts are safely buried.

There's no easy sleep after such a film, and at daybreak I was still tossing fitfully when my bedside phone rang—and then the whip, the shriek, the breathless voice rushing through all sorts of details faster than my mind could register them.

"Professor Klinkowitz," sang an eerily high-pitched and inflected voice that I'd never heard before, speaking in a heavy Polish accent that my drowsiness was turning into Transylvanian *à la* Bela Lugosi. "This is Jerzy Kosinski in New Haven; will you please come and see me *tonight*!"

"NO!" I gasped in reply, pure terror making the same judgment that cool reason would.

"I may have to leave the country very suddenly," the voice protested, even more rushed now, "with no advance notice at all. Perhaps I might never return, who knows? I could be dead tomorrow, as the saying goes. So please, we should do the interview very soon while we still have the chance!"

Quite unhappily I agreed, and with books and notecards and emotions all in disarray, I changed my reservations and flew to New York, where my friends Lynn and Mel Bendett drove me up to New Haven. By the time I'd dropped my bags at the Sheraton, it was almost 9:00 P.M.—a dark and windy night, cold for early November, the streets deserted, Davenport College (where Kosinski lived) frightening and menacing in its Gothic gimcrackery. Past an iron gate, up the narrow winding stairs to the fourth-floor top: at any moment I expected arms to come reaching out of the walls and blood to start pouring from the ceiling—two tricks which Polanski's film had played on me and which I'd never forget.

But the Jerzy Kosinski who answered the door was from another world: warmly gracious, anxious for my comfort, and, with practiced calm, ready to offer a cozy chair, a few imported beers, and answers to my silliest questions. All I had to do, he explained, was sign over the copyright to anything he said on tape. The request came as a surprise, but as a novice interviewer I presumed it to be kosher and—after coming this far—gladly signed on the dotted line. He glanced at my signature and said, "Klinkowitz—that's *Klinkiewicz*, Polish, right?" I said yes, my great-grandfather had changed it to avoid Bismarck's infamous draft (or so my relatives would always claim).

So we sat back and talked for an hour, my tape recorder and his backup system (as he called it) getting every word: his muteness as a child; the escape from Poland, accomplished by forging documents, creating references, and finally conducting a mock bureaucratic war over his exit visa, all to make it look good; his first days as an expatriate in New York, hard work at menial jobs, and so forth. Kosinski at his desk. Myself in the easy chair—sumptuous leather, fireplace at one elbow, leaded windows at the other, with Davenport's stupid gargoyles peering in. All the horror was safely locked outside.

Then at 10:30 P.M., the phone rang. Kosinski snapped off both his tape recorder and mine and, after his first "hello" in English, spoke on the phone in rudimentary French for a few moments before rushing on in Polish. After a minute, he covered the mouthpiece and spoke to me, ever the courteous host worried about the comfort of his guest. "You must excuse me," he begged, "but the conversation I am about to have will be in a language other than that in which we have been speaking."

Then back to the phone and into Polish, a language that I could not understand, even to catch occasional cognates and guess at what was being discussed. But neither did Kosinski leave me in the dark. After nearly twenty minutes of talk, his companion Kiki brought us more beer; Jerzy paused, excused himself to the caller, and told us who it was.

"It's my brother in Warsaw," he announced.

Kiki looked worried.

"You see," Kosinski said, turning to me, "my mother in Poland is very ill. I was told just recently that she had three, perhaps six, months to live. That's why I expect to leave suddenly: I wish to see my mother and she wishes to see me, but I cannot return to Poland, for obvious reasons." With this he gestured to the tape on which he'd documented his story of illegal exit. "So it has been arranged," he continued, "that we will each fly to Amsterdam, a free city. That's where we'll meet," he said, turning back to Kiki, "Tuesday."

"Is that what your brother says?" she asked.

"More," Kosinski added. He was now staring straight ahead, speaking more to himself than to either of us. "I was told to look into the matter of disposing a body in Amsterdam."

Kiki gasped.

"The flight, the doctors say, will kill Mama."

Any further pedestrian questions that I may have planned for that Sunday night deserted me. Kosinski quickly concluded his call and reached forward, tripping the record button on each machine, and answered the question that I had asked him nearly half an hour before.

Our interview continued, stretching three more hours into the early morning, and concluded with a second session the next day, when I was supposed to be having lunch with Tom Stats, a kid from my old block in Milwaukee who was presently a drama student at Yale; I saw Tom later that day, packed my notes together, and trained back to my friends' home in New York with a briefcase full of tasty Kosinski stories that I was eager to show and tell. After three painstaking revisions and a foolish submission to *The Atlantic* (where Michael Curtis rejected it as press agentry), the piece appeared as scheduled in Joe David Bellamy's *fiction international* and was published again in his university press collection, *The New Fiction: Interviews with Innovative American Writers*. It was, I can say without vanity, one of the meatier discussions in the book, since everything took on a more serious tone after that scary, traumatizing phone call. My questions lost their silliness and gained some depth: my first impressions so rudely shocked, I had gone beyond feelings of fear and beery camaraderie and stood suddenly in perfect awe of the man.

I left New Haven thinking that I'd had a private audience with the likes of Henry Kissinger or the Pope—or, better yet, with a combination of the two. My grandchildren would hear the story, as would theirs, for by then Jerzy Kosinski would surely be enshrined as one of the greatest writers of all time. The phone call in the midst of my nightmares, the hurried flight east, the comfortable study into which flashed that transatlantic message from the Polish night—I had been privileged to witness the making of a myth! What testimony to give: Kosinski was larger than life.

The myth began to crack a bit when I tested it out on Kosinski's friends. Zjizslav Njader, a Polish Conrad scholar who visited my university that year, said that he'd known Kosinski since his first months as an émigré in New York and scoffed at the notion of Jerzy's inability to return home. Under such circumstances as a mother's impending death, Njader claimed, there would be no problem at all.

"Those Polish bureaucrats don't care that Kosinski left so many years ago," he chided me. "Kosinski must certainly know the type: they're a bunch of old sentimentalists. He'd say his mother was dying and they'd cry their eyes out as they let him in and let him out again."

But this, I told myself, was just politics. Njader, as a Pole living in a friendlier Eastern Europe and enjoying free and frequent travel back and forth between the two blocs, no doubt had too rosy a view of things. The myth demanded the image of Kosinski at the border, pulled one way by trench-coated government agents and the other by freedom fight-ers—a scenario favored by American audiences since the Hungarian uprisings of 1956. I myself had been witness to part of the Kosinski legend, which reminded me of heroic Fa-ther Goulet, an escapee from Budapest who had joined our parish in the Milwaukee suburbs sometime late in '56 after God knows what tortures, and that was how I wanted to see the legend.

And see it that way I did, until it turned against me. With-in a few years, I'd expanded the phone call story into a full-fledged after-dinner entertainment and was putting it through the paces for friends of Professor Ihab Hassan in Milwaukee—a divertissement before the coffee, cognac, and cigars. This was, after all, the perfect audience, for Ihab and Sally Hassan had been colleagues of a younger Kosinski at Wesleyan years before. Surely, they too were partakers of the myth, and so I told my story, expecting gasps, wonder, and confirmation of my awe. Instead, I got knowing looks and a few disconcerting chuckles.

"How remarkable," Sally said after a few moments, imitating my own concluding rapture. "To think of that little room in New Haven, and from across the dark Atlantic that startling telephone call from Poland, a glimpse of the horror beyond all horrors!"

She smiled at Ihab, who continued in the same gently mocking tone. "How even more remarkable," he said, "and perhaps more likely, to think of that phone call coming from across the Yale campus, from Jerzy's graduate assistant who'd been instructed, 'Ring me up at 10:30 tonight and let me talk Polish to you for half an hour so we can scare the pants off Klinkowitz'!"

So which was the truth? Jerzy Kosinski, champion of life, survivor of the holocaust and later calamities, caught in the most maddening and pathetic of international circumstances as he flies his mother out of Poland to almost certain death? Or Jerzy Kosinski, manipulating an interviewer, as he must manipulate them all, into just the awe-struck mood that he wanted for this talk? As with the polo story, you can take your choice. Kosinski has insured that, at the bottom line of truth, where he lives secure, where *he* reveals the secrets, you and I will never know.

———————————————

Circles within circles: the mother's-death story eventually made its way into *Blind Date*, published six years after the experience that he'd put me through. Other stories, both public and private, popped up in this book: fellow novelist Jim Sloan's tale, for example, told at the MLA, about Kosinski learning English mainly because his various Slavic languages lacked the proper vocabulary for gentle sexual seduction; Kosinski's own talk-show routine describing a friend speaking "Esquimaux" in a Parisian cafe and being assaulted by two burly Soviets who assumed that they'd been targeted for insult by the scatological Russian which had in fact been spoken; the trick Kosinski told me about using a garden hose to squirt horse cabs along 6th Avenue from his eighteenth-floor balcony while the doormen below transformed the inexplicable event into meteorological myth; his ploys for cutting through bureaucratic indolence and for speeding letters through the lethargic mails, plus news stories of his involvement with such celebrity authors as Reza Baraheni, Jacques Monod, and Leopold Sedar Senghor. All nice little narratives. But now they were confusing because they'd first been reported as facts involving Kosinski and were now being presented as fiction.

Another *Blind Date* tale that was apparently drawn from life was the experience of being kidnapped by a maniacal taxi driver. For me the effect was double, as the event happened to Kosinski at the Los Angeles International Airport on the day after his speech at the University of Northern Iowa (where I was now teaching)—or so he claimed in a phone call to my colleague Dan Cahill the following afternoon. He then told the same story on "The Johnny Carson Show" that night.

Climaxing the book was a lengthy dramatization, blow by sickening blow, of the Sharon Tate murders. Here the names were changed, but the fictional personalities were clear transparencies for six of Kosinski's closest friends. Unlike the novel's other scenes from life, Jerzy himself had not been there, and so, like Nick Carraway recounting Gatsby's death, he had to work entirely from imagination. And as in *Gatsby*, the results were stunning, resulting in some of Kosinski's best prose on record.

Why did he use these stories in his novel? Or, better yet, why had he told them as truth if they were later to appear as fiction? "To try them out on an audience," he advised. But that seemed too simple: in the fictional versions, most of these tales took on added dimensions and played more games still. For example, *Blind Date*'s taxi cab story develops just as it did in Kosinski's televised autobiography, right up to one crucial and climactic point, just as does the mother's-death tale. One can only guess that Kosinski is inviting the knowledgeable reader to play along, implying that the parallels between his life and his hero's are harmless and even amusing. Those charming anecdotes end on little upbeats, in quaint moral lessons, or simply laughs. Senghor mistaking Kosinski for a bellboy: cute. Baraheni freed from a Savak prison by Kosinski's intervention: an impressive happy ending.

But as in Polanski's *Repulsion*, we are being conditioned. For right at the end of *Blind Date*'s taxi story—which to this point has been matching Kosinski's "Johnny Carson Show" account step by step—comes the unthinkable: the cabbie is outmaneuvered by his intended victim and is most brutally and sadistically murdered. Nor does the fictional story of the protagonist's mother end with her death: instead, we return to the earlier days of her life spent in blissfully incestuous union with her son. Are these concluding touches autobiographical as well? That's what Kosinski knows we're too shocked to ask, although he's tricked us into wondering.

This is, after all, how the *The Painted Bird* works. We read along, perhaps beyond our depth, because the uninviting topics of psychotic mayhem have been safely contained in perfectly acceptable prose. If we can read this far, we think, everything must be okay. At which point Kosinski springs his trap, shocking us with previously unimaginable horror that less skillful writing would have let degenerate into titillation or farce.

The stories that Kosinski tells in life, whether true or false, serve the same purpose. Their author reveals them so that they will be talked about in all their contradictions, and those contradictions are the key part of the tale. Catching Kosinski in an occasional slip-up only makes the genius of his behavior easier to admire: like the action of his novels, his life story may be unverifiable, but it is never boring, and his rewriting of the past reveals his absolute commitment to the present as our only firm reality. As I met more people who'd known Kosinski earlier in life, these inconsistencies became more frequent and more strikingly transparent. Zjizslav Njader had told me that Kosinski's claim to have mastered photography simply as a way of facilitating escape to the West was a fiction. "He desperately wanted to be a photographer all the time," Njader claimed.

"But Kosinski says he threw away his cameras when he landed at Idlewild in 1957," I protested.

"Listen," came the reply. "I remember a whole week back then driving Kosinski all over New York City and Long Island, from Eastman Kodak to every other photo outfit in the book, as he sought work in photography or photographic chemistry."

Was he indeed an associate professor at the Polish Academy of Sciences in Warsaw? That was how he translated the rank of *aspirant*, his formal title.

"Nonsense," Njader replied. "*Aspirant* means 'graduate assistant.' "

On my visit to Poland in fall of 1979, I was further deluged with curious stories about Kosinski: how *The Painted Bird* was

allegedly plagiarized from Polish sociological books and journals; how *Being There* was supposedly cribbed from a prewar
novel by Tadeusz Dołyga-Mostowicz called *The Career of Ni-
kodemia Dyzmy*, a book so popular in Poland that it became a
successful film and has in recent years been the basis for a TV
serial. More pointedly, several critics not at all hostile to his
work assured me that Kosinski's tale of forged documents
and surreptitious flight sounded like a needless fabrication.
"He left late in 1957," they said. "That was during a six-
month thaw in relations with the West: you can look up the
announcements from the Party Congresses here and in Mos-
cow. Visas were very easy to get; going West was encouraged. Kosinski would have had nothing to worry about—a
cyanide capsule under his tongue, indeed!"

Admittedly, this took some of the drama out of Kosinski's
emigration. Looking back, one sees that *The Future Is Ours,
Comrade*, *No Third Path*, and even *The Painted Bird* were published with right wing endorsements; perhaps the marketing
of these books, like Kosinski's great escape story, pandered to
Cold War sentiments. In any event, Kosinski had fashioned
his own American myth out of his daring flight to freedom—
a flight in the style that Americans admired in countless other
escapes from Hungary, East Germany, and other Warsaw
Pact states. Without real danger, his story would lack mythic
proportion.

Which may be a clue to understanding Kosinski's fabula-
tive existence. The novels, he may feel, need a myth surrounding them, and he's been careful, furthermore, to keep
that mythology consistent with the changes in American political sensibility, from Cold War hostility through detente
and back again to rambunctious anti-Communism. Hence,
the excited phone calls which accompany each new book. On
matters of lesser substance, I've caught him in embarrassing

contradictions, in midstream changes in the hype with which he accompanies each successive work. For years, he'd cultivated a rather flamboyant pose in not allowing his novels to be filmed. Cinema was a manipulative medium, Kosinski would claim, a product of the American collective that he so despised. His books demanded the activation of the reader's imagination, while movies imposed the director's design. His books were internal affairs, encodings of language, while film was of course external and visual. These were familiar principles in his essays and interviews, and therefore when he phoned me with the news that *Being There* was going Hollywood I cited his principles for him.

"I *must* film this book," he said with some impatience, "because I feel America needs to know its message," and then he went on to describe a very intricate approach to filming which would keep his earlier principles intact. "All the minor characters, all the supporting roles," he reported with great relish, "will be played by well-known actors—so well known that they themselves are institutions, just like the ones that *Being There* employs." Okay. "The role of Chance, however, will be played by a complete unknown, a new actor to whom the audience can have no predictable response." About this he went on in great detail: a "nationwide talent search" for the Great Unknown Actor, "filming in secret" so that the fan magazines could create no public expectations which would interfere with Kosinski's perfect blank of a cinematic protagonist. And so forth.

When the filming did get underway, Kosinski himself was the center of a well-orchestrated publicity campaign in the Washington, D.C., papers, where the movie's location scenes were shot. Moreover, magazines everywhere quoted Kosinski as saying that Peter Sellers—who'd been cast as Chance—had nailed down the role eight years before. Sellers, of course, was a great mimic; critics loved to say how his own personality could never be known, so thoroughly did he assume the parodic roles he played. So this part of Kosinski's myth was intact. But for the first time, I'd been privileged to be standing not in awe but somewhere behind the scenes, witnessing a few last-minute set and cast changes before the curtain rose on The Great Kosinski, new and improved for the 1980s—just as his stridently right wing image had been jettisoned for the later 1960s.

Any day now, I expect the phone to ring and to be danced upon his puppet-master's string once more. Will I ask about these latest contradictions—contradictions with which the *Times* and the *Voice* are still struggling? No: you don't quibble with Henry Kissinger, the Pope, or Jerzy Kosinski. Here at the University of Northern Iowa, my friend Dan Cahill can point out odd textual inconsistencies which contradict certain biographical myths. My colleague Jim Martin can show me how Kosinski, contrary to the claims on which his "necessary English" was based, did in fact publish a stateside book in Polish, *Socjologia Amerykańska* (New York: Polski Instytut Naukowy w Amercye—no copyright, but listed in the firm's backlist as a 1962 publication), which anthologizes essays written in the objective style of the Columbia University Sociology Department, where Kosinski was working on a Ph.D. (and which is not at all the subjective, even lyrical style of his own collective behavior books being published under the name "Joseph Novak"). And my old Marquette officemate Jim Hiduke can show me how the rhetoric of Kosinski's public life has been a twenty-five-year struggle to take America's penchant for making fetishes out of her authors and turn it back against herself—and to Kosinski's own survivalist benefit!

But who really cares about such arcane matters of muddled autobiography—matters which, at this writing, have generated both a full-fledged press war in New York and devastating parodies published as fiction by *The New Yorker* and satire by *The Nation*. As far as novelists and literary critics should be concerned, these are circles within circles, and the real Kosinski story will never be known—a fact which this master fictionist has been teaching me ever since that spooky night at Yale eleven years ago.

Thinking back to Kosinski's interview of me that evening, I recall that my great-grandfather changed Klinkiewicz to Klinkowitz in 1870; maybe he thought Bismarck would like it better. He was a pretender, like the grandfather of my friend and colleague Jim Bittner. Jim's grandfather changed the family name from Bitnar and also claimed that he was dodging the Prussian army—and not in fact the Czech police, all of which would make for a much lesser myth. Which am I, Klinkiewicz or Klinkowitz? Who is Jim, Bittner or Bitnar? Who is Kosinski? Does it matter? Yes, because it gives us all something to write about, to tell stories about. To tell stories is to generate secrets, and that is the central point of Kosinski's life and art.

At Home with Dan Wakefield

1. Opening credits over long shot: Eastern Airlines shuttle descending into Boston's Logan International Airport.

Voice-over of a telephone conversation—

The Critic: "Dan? Jerry Klinkowitz. I'm in New York, and these shuttle connections are going to make it easy. I saw Kurt yesterday, and this afternoon I'll finish up with Barthelme and Kosinski. So you'll see me at either seven or six, depending which plane I catch. I don't even need a ticket!"

The Author: "Sure, Jerry, those are nice connections, Logan's great that way. It's a pretty short ride over here to the Hill, too, but watch out for the cab drivers—I swear to God every one of them in Boston is crazy."

2. Medium shot of the arrivals concourse with the critic being shunted from cab to cab. *Zoom back* to traffic warden explaining to the next waiting passenger, "I told that guy nobody's gonna want to take him to Revere Street! These hackies pay a buck to sit in line for three hours, they want a fare to the suburbs at least."

3. Close shot of Dan Wakefield at the door of his Beacon Hill town house. *Zoom back* to show the critic emerging from taxi with his travel bag. *Opening credits* conclude.

4. Medium shot of group sharing talk and cocktails in the author's book-lined living room. Present are the author, the author's housemate, the critic, critic Shaun O'Connell and his wife, plus Mark Vonnegut. Shots immediately following shift with the speaker.

The Author: "So what's new with Kurt?"

The Critic: "He says hello, was pleased that Mark would be by. He told me you're the real literary host up here, the closest thing Boston has to an intelligent social center so writers can keep in touch. Like that piece in *Boston* magazine said. This house is perfect."

The Author: "With all those sudden royalties it was buy property or go bust for taxes. I almost put it into a boat, a good-sized sloop we could live out of at the marina. But then sanity intervened and here I am on the Hill."

The Critic: "Royalties from *Going All the Way?*"

The Author: "Some of them. That was the first book of mine I'd ever seen in supermarket racks. So I knew it would be paying good. What's really amazing is that when the movies bought *Starting Over* for Burt Reynolds and Jill Clayburgh, it turned out to mean less than all those lovely paperbacks in the grocery marts and drugstores. So we are still a literate nation."

Shaun O'Connell: "How long had you been 'homeless'?"

The Author: "Oh, all the way back to student days, at Columbia, after leaving Indianapolis."

The Critic: "Kurt Vonnegut country. Did you know his work then, the magazine stuff, back in the 1950s?"

5. Long shot of a street in Indianapolis, *zoom in* to *interior shot* of a barbershop decorated in early 1950s style. *Voice-over* of the author—The first time I read anything by Kurt Vonnegut, I was sitting in a barbershop in Indianapolis, leafing through a dog-eared copy of *The Saturday Evening Post* while waiting to have my favorite barber give me one of those kind of haircuts that prompted jocular fellows to quip, "Hey, I see you got your ears set out! Har, har, har." (People said "Har, har, har" then to let you know something was funny: it was one of those doldrum years like 1953 when people seemed especially self-conscious and wanted to be what was called "one of the boys.")

6. Wandering shots of Indianapolis environs to accompany the following commentary. *Voice-over* of the critic—Just the thing Kurt was writing about back then, though he was eight-hundred miles east on Cape Cod. And here you are in Boston, writing a novel twenty years later about two young men trying to figure some way out of all that. Were things back home in Indiana really that claustrophobic?

The Author: "Only when you got out and saw the difference. As I said in the introductory part to my collection of journalistic pieces, *Between the Lines,* the finest tribute I can pay my old block is to say that I firmly believe it would have driven an inquiring sociologist into some other profession. Its breadwinners were not all white color or blue, its families neither all American-born nor all foreign-born, and at least among the kids—and so, to my knowledge—there was no consciousness of 'class' or social status. We knew that outside The Block there were rich people who lived in bigger houses than we did, but that did not concern us any more than things we knew to exist outside, such as Eskimos, elephants, and elevated trains (the latter phenomena we heard could be found in far-off Chicago)."

7. Close shots of critic and author in Beacon Hill living room, camera following conversation.

The Critic: "And *Between the Lines,* published in 1966, was how you met Kurt Vonnegut."

The Author: "Yes, I asked the publisher to send a set of galleys to Vonnegut in case he would be so kind as to want to make a comment about it. I got back a wonderful letter from him about the book and my autobiographical preface about growing up in Indianapolis, life on The Block, and how my dreams of athletic stardom were smashed when I found out that I could not break the seven-minute mile. He confessed that he, too, had been unable to break the seven-minute mile and that he had had so many of the same teachers and same experiences as I described that, as he put it, 'I almost feel that there shouldn't be two of us.'"

The Critic: "I can see why. Yesterday in New York, Kurt said you're like the little brother he always wanted but never had."

8. Close shot of Kurt Vonnegut in his New York town house, paging through Wakefield's *Going All the Way* and addressing the camera.

Vonnegut: "Yeah, I helped Dan with the title. He originally was calling it *Sons and Mothers* but his publisher, Seymour Lawrence, who is also my publisher, thought this would be too confusing, as there are so many other books with similar titles, such as *Sons and Lovers, Mothers and Sons,* and so on. So we all tried to think of titles, and I came up with the perfectly unacceptable suggestion of *Getting Laid in Indianapolis.*

"Going All the Way is about what hell it is to be oversexed in Indianapolis, and why so many oversexed people run away from there. It is also about the narrowness and dimness of many lives out that way. And I guarantee you this: Wakefield himself, having written this book, can never go home again. From now on, he will have to watch the 500-mile Speedway race on television."

9. Wandering shots of Indianapolis locations keyed to Vonnegut's *voice-over*—

Wakefield's reportage of life in Middle America, as one might expect, is gruesomely accurate and enchanting. His sex-addled fools tool their parents' automobiles through a vast pinball machine whose bumpers and kickers are strip joints and taverns and gas stations and golf driving ranges and hamburger stands. They seek whorehouses, which, it turns out, have been closed for years.

They return home periodically to their smug and vapid parents, grumpily declining to say where they've been. Their stomachs, already churning with hamburgers and beer, twist even more grotesquely when their parents want to know when they are going to settle down to nice jobs and nice wives and nice houses in Indianapolis.

10. Close shot of the cover of the paperback edition Vonnegut has been holding, with his blurb visible: "The truest and funniest sex novel any American will ever write—Kurt Vonnegut, Jr." *Voice-over* of the Critic and the Author in dialogue—

The Critic: *"Going All the Way* is perfectly framed, a nice start for your trilogy that continues with *Starting Over* and concludes with *Home Free. . . ."*

The Author: "Yes . . ."

The Critic: "Especially how it begins and ends with Sonny wondering where his 'real' life is. Coming back home after his army service he thinks to himself that he's at 'the start of a whole new part of his life—the "real" part . . . nosing into the future, unlimited.' Of course after three-hundred pages, he and his buddy Gunner haven't progressed one bit, as they're still thinking about the future. . . ."

11. Medium shot in the Beacon Hill living room of the discussion underway, which the camera follows (as the critic reads from his paperback)—

The Critic: "Recovering from the auto wreck, Sonny sneaks out of the hospital and reexperiences the Indianapolis street, where for a moment 'It seemed as if everything was bathed in a soft gold light, like a blessing. It was just a moment but it gave Sonny a sudden sense of joy that seemed to spread through his whole being.' He recalls how the best parts of his life have been just such moments, which 'made you feel completely alive, reminded you of being alive, and Sonny wondered if perhaps that's what "real life" was after all—those moments. He didn't find it depressing, but felt perhaps it meant that his real life had been going on all the time, that the moments were to remind him of it and let him feel it.' So perhaps Sonny's quest had been for what he's had all along?"

The Author: "I suppose so, but I wonder if he'll ever know it."

The Critic: "You mean you can't go home again, even if you've never left?"

The Author: "I have some proof of that. One afternoon Eve called me down from the study to meet some visitors who'd rung the doorbell. It was two young men who'd driven all the way from Indianapolis to compliment me for writing the story of their still-young lives. Here they were, I thought, Sonny and Gunner, thinking they'd found the answer at my kitchen door a thousand miles from home."

12. Medium shot, moving to close, as the author and critic walk up Revere Street and down the other side of Beacon Hill to Charles Street and the Public Gardens. As conversation continues, they settle into a restaurant on Beacon Street for lunch—

The Critic: "*Going All the Way* is 1970, right? And the book which settled you into your Boston home. But by the time of 1973, with *Starting Over,* you seem ready to tear it all down, for your hero Potter starts out homeless."

The Author: "Yes, it begins with the fact of his divorce. Everyone says he's lucky—that's the first line—because he doesn't have children."

The Critic: "Well, he seems at home quickly enough—that's the nice use you make of Boston and Cambridge: the parks and restaurants and little social crowds here and there take him in. John Updike has written about it much the same way in the years since—"

The Author: "—Some of those stories in *Problems*—"

The Critic: "Yes, which he wrote while living in that small room here on Beacon Street before he remarried. 'The wives always get the houses' is one line I remember from that collection."

13. Long to medium roving shots of Boston environs, following the pattern of shots 6 and 9 of Indianapolis, to accompany the critic's reading in *voice-over*—

Those are my favorite passages of *Starting Over,* where you catch the sense of these detached people moving through the city: "He walked a lot. Every morning he walked the eight blocks to Harvard Square, where he bought the *Boston Globe* and the *New York Times* and went to breakfast at a cafeteria on Brattle Street where you could sit and pore over the papers, refill your coffee, and not be rushed into eating up and moving on. After breakfast he walked down to the Charles and strolled along the banks. Occasionally he found a game of touch football he could get into. That was one of the best things. The running and jumping and throwing and blocking that brought sweat to the body also washed the mind clean. He would walk home pleasantly aching and exhausted, take long showers, get into his bathrobe, and settle down to read. He hadn't read so much in years—not only books for his courses, but novels in paperback whose titles he had bandied about at cocktail parties with the bluff assurance he got from culling descriptions in reviews. Around midnight he would flick on the tube and burrow into bed for the talk shows and late movies that, with enough Scotch, usually got him to sleep (p. 25)."

That's what I like about *Starting Over:* these characters who manage to work out their homey little life routines without benefit of a real home. When he meets Marilyn, we find that her routines are much the same, after one trying incident fleeing home to pop two Valium and head for bed.

14. Close shot of the author and critic back at lunch, camera following their conversation—

The Critic: "In their detachment, I sense a style of freedom, maybe what Sonny and Gunner were looking for. After all, Potter and Marilyn are *adults,* and they're free to do whatever they want, even if it doesn't add up to much. *Starting Over* seems just that, one of many re-starts that will eventually add up only to life's moving along."

The Author: "The book ends with the same line as its beginning."

The Critic: "Yes, and I remember the scene it frames: Potter getting married again, everyone at the ceremony telling him how lucky he is, and just at this very moment he's looking somewhere else, at a fetching young woman prancing about just out of the picture."

15. Long shot of the author and critic walking back up Beacon Hill—

The Critic: "Following *Starting Over,* you interrupted your fictional trilogy with a book on soap operas, *All Her Children*—"

The Author: "It was really just about the most successful soap opera, 'All My Children.' I'd been caught up in it as a fan myself, and began to wonder, What is it that so compels millions of intelligent Americans to watch this story each day?"

16. Close shot of a television screen, which shows scenes from an episode of "All My Children" as the critic continues in *voice-over*—

Can a sweet young girl from a Colorado mining town find happiness as the wife of an English baron? That's quite a question, but no less imposing than the one which follows: Can the type of television show that asks this question hold the largest audience there has ever been for any type of story?

17. Medium shot of Dan Wakefield sitting in his kitchen, a TV set playing "All My Children" visible behind him and to the side—

The Author: "It has been socially acceptable for housewives to watch soap operas. But the popular image of the sort of housewife who would actually watch them is a gross composite of the cartoon 'Hazel the Maid' and Shirley Booth playing the slatternly heroine of *Come Back, Little Sheba.* But if

you look at the stories themselves, you'll find no such stereotypes: they're about the kind of people living when we were,
people like we knew or might possibly know. If this is a 'soap
opera existence,' consider how little of real pertinence makes
it onto the prime time television screens in such milky shows
as *The Waltons* or *Little House on the Prairie.* "

18. Close shot of television screen again showing "All My Children" as the author's *voice-over* continues—
   In less specific, but more pervasive ways, I was getting
from the TV soap operas a more accurate feel of American
society, in tones of thought and talk and dress, than I could
find in most newspapers and magazines, and certainly more
so than in any of the laugh-tracked, sickly sweet family fantasy dramas of nighttime "adult" viewing. I described this to a
friend, who replied, "You mean it's just like life." I certainly
think so, and that's why viewers are drawn to it.

19. Medium shot of the critic addressing the author in the
kitchen—
   The Critic: "I see; that's why you devoted so much study
to see how these lifelike stories were made. Just like good literary realism, it's quite an artificial process: how these programs make the most money in TV from the smallest bud-
gets, how their intricate plots must be woven about the
limitations of four sets, no more than two dozen actors and
actresses, and a daily taping schedule that keeps a scant few
days ahead of a five-day-a-week, fifty-two-weeks-a-year seri-
alization. It really makes for a compelling story of a compelling story."
   The Author: "That's what one of the cast told me. 'Isn't it
fun?' she asked me as I watched a taping. 'All of us are

hooked on it, too. We can't wait to find out what happens next!' "

20. Medium shot of the author and the critic emerging from a cab at Logan Airport's departure concourse. The author is paying the taxi driver—
    The Author: "See how easy that was, Jerry?"

21. Long shot of the author and critic in the departure lounge; scene of several airline counters, flight boards changing, departures to various American cities being announced.

22. Close shot of critic as he settles into a coffee shop chair; in the background departure announcements can still be heard—
    The Critic: "This sounds like an itinerary for your novel *Home Free.* That's from 1977, almost a complete decade after your cross-country tour in journalism, *Supernation at Peace and War,* which covered just about everything—"

23. Close shot of jacket of *Supernation at Peace and War,* the subtitle of which reads *Being Certain Observations, Depositions, Testimonies, and Graffiti Gathered on a One-Man Fact-and-Fantasy-Finding Tour of the Most Powerful Nation in the World* in whimsical script. *Voice-over* of the author—
    Yes, that was the year Robert Kennedy and Martin Luther King were assassinated, protest against the Vietnam War was at new highs, we'd been shocked by the Tet offensive, Lyndon Johnson declined to seek a second elected term, and here's what I'd learn from the woman in the street: "You know what concerns me most at this moment?" she asked me

out in Indiana. "Whether to get my son a finished desk or an unfinished desk for his study."

24. Medium shot of author and critic in the coffee shop, camera following their conversation—

The Critic: "Just like soap opera—not the maudlin atten-tion-grabbing superstories, but the little truths which make up life while the chronicles of history thunder on?"

The Author: "There's much of the little stuff like that in *Home Free.*"

The Critic: "Indeed. I wonder how many people fifty years from now will remember the mid-1960s as not just the Vietnam protest years but also as the time when a new foot-ball league grew and successfully merged with the old one, rock music acquired a country flavor, blacks appeared in TV commercials for the first time, and the nation rediscovered romance.

"Of course, being a protagonist often blinds one to this. I keep recalling Sonny and Gunner wondering when their 'real life' was going to start, and Potter always looking for the next affair before the present one was even established. In *Home Free* your hero Gene is part of the times for a while—ac-tivism, communal life, the Beatles, and so forth—but its cen-trifugal force spins him off and out. That's where the novel's best parts begin, when he's cut loose to wander up to Maine, out to Iowa, and finally to the physical edge of things in Cali-fornia."

The Author: "And he's so lost. You'll recall how he ex-plains his adventures to himself—"

25. Wandering long shot of street scene in Venice, California, emphasizing waste and directionlessness, as a flight departure for "Los Angeles International Airport" is announced and the author continues to read in a *voice-over*—

He'd walked into it like walking up the aisle of a movie and melting into the screen and becoming a part of the picture, the story, finding out what happened as you went along, knowing from the beginning how it would end but not when. Then he'd be standing on the stage feeling silly and strange with the screen dark and the houselights on. Bright. He'd be blinking, trying to find his way out. In the meantime this was life.

26. Long shot of author saying farewell to critic at airport gate—

    The Author: "Keep in touch."

    The Critic: "That's what phones are for."

27. Long shot across hood of automobile pulling off the highway to enter Geneseo, Illinois; camera shifts to side shots, taking in the passing storefronts and lawns as the following telephone conversation proceeds in *voice-over*—

    The Critic: "Dan? This is Jerry Klinkowitz. Somebody just told me that you're back home from Hollywood."

    The Author: "Yes. After two and a half years. It was great for the series—'James at 15'—and I did a TV movie too. But you know, I can only write novels at home!"

    The Critic: "We're driving East later this month and wonder if you'll be in Boston?"

    The Author: "Of course. Do you have the new novel?"

    The Critic: *"Under the Apple Tree,* yes. I really like it. You told me its setting, 'Birney, Illinois,' is based on Geneseo. You know, that's right along our route. But what happened to Indianapolis, to Indiana? I thought this was your big 'home' novel after that trilogy of heroes off on false quests."

28. Medium shot of the author, the critic, and the critic's wife in the author's living room—still on Beacon Hill, but now an apartment on Mount Vernon Street on the opposite slope. Camera follows conversation—

The Author: "You see, part of my childhood in Indianapolis was in a part of town still somewhat out in the country. To actually base the novel there would entail a lot of awkward explanations. But a few years ago, one of my old writing students of the University of Iowa wrote me to say he'd taken a high school teaching job in Geneseo, Illinois, and that here was the location I needed, a small town where some of those early 1940s wartime characteristics were still evident."

The Critic: "It really does seem a perfect novel of manners for those years. Did you really go back and look up all those old *Life* magazines with the patriotic ads and citizen-readiness advice?"

29. Close shots of magazine covers and stories being described, aircraft spotters' handbooks, block warden paraphernalia, etc. Author's *voice-over*—

Of course, I remembered quite a bit of it, but I checked to make sure I was not exaggerating in nostalgically comic recall. In fact, there's another novel to be written which I could set within the magazine styles of the postwar years: how our mission as victors was to civilize and rehabilitate the Japanese, to teach them American principles of business and industry (which they've now mastered better than us!), and to beef them up with a rich diet of hamburgers and milkshakes, certainly to get them off things like raw fish and seaweed— just the very things that are popular here now!

30. Medium shot back in the author's apartment. Camera follows conversation, breaking occasionally for close-ups spliced in of book covers and jacket photos framed on the walls—

The Critic: "Those are the little touches I like so much, because they anchor the story so solidly. After all, your lost protagonist, little Artie Garber seems so solidly, so happily at home, because he has all these materials, all these signs by which to locate himself: scrap iron drives, war bond stamps, action comics—plus that whole idolization of his older brother, who actually serves—"

The Author: "And who is of course psychologically devastated by the experience, in a way which Artie, in his ten-year-old's world of fantasies, just can't understand."

The Critic: "Except at the very end—"

The Author: "And that's when he knows he's not a kid anymore."

31. Medium shot, panning past the framed book covers and jacket photos, toward the critic and his wife departing. The author stands as a host giving benediction, as the conversation concludes—

The Critic: "Dan, there's one last question: After ten years of messing around with experimental fiction, pushing all these innovations to their logical and illogical extremes, what am I doing back here congratulating you for your literary realism, your triumph in the novel of manners?"

The Author: "Jerry, I have a question for you: Where have you been so long? Welcome home!"

Postcards from Tom Glynn

PREPARE FOR THE onslaught. On August 18, Patricia & Kids arrive in Cedar Falls after motoring from West Coast. And I arrive from the East. Then one day later Jon Baumbach & Clarence Major arrive. Should be big fiction gathering in Iowa. Don't worry about room. We have tent. Can sleep in your back yard. Looking forward to seeing you. My first meeting with Clarence Major too and I am looking forward to that. We leave for Michigan August 21.

—7/19/78

Tom flies in a day earlier, August 17, on a warm and quiet Iowa night. His Ozark connection from Chicago lands at 8:00 P.M., and the sun is well down within the hour. The quiet unnerves him.

"Can't we get some kids to walk by with transistors?" he asks. "Don't you have pachango music in Iowa? Doesn't this quiet bother you?"

For all his Chicago heritage and New York/Brooklyn/Prospect Heights savvy, Tom Glynn chose the deeper quiet of upstate Adirondack, New York for his novel *Temporary Sanity* (Fiction Collective, 1976).

The book is about a life we can easily recognize but rarely attend to—the life of throw-away people in a beautiful but thrown-away part of the world, who are made real to us by the way Glynn makes them speak, think, and dream.

Compared to his innovative colleagues, hellbent for abstract expressionism, Glynn's book reads a bit like realism. But realism from the brush of Chagall. Everything is credible yet still *magic*.

Please consider this a strong invitation to come up. We have electricity, a well, a pump, and an outhouse. We've got an old backwoods bar, a waterfall where we go swimming, and starry nights that will blow the top of your head off . . . sometimes in August we get northern lights that can really scatter your mind.

—8/1/76

"Jarrel didn't say nothing the whole way down." A subtle touch of bad grammar, but enough to let us know all of *Temporary Sanity* will be a story of language. Syntax askew, reality just a touch off kilter—these are the tonal shades of Tom Glynn's fiction. "Always a good idea to have a stick of TNT on you. Never know when you'd need it," Jarrel thinks, and by page three we're ready to agree, since Glynn has us thinking in the rhythms of these people's lives.

Pat and the kids roll in the next noon, just as we're clearing the dishes, and Tom has his Brooklyn clamor again. Brendan, Siobahn, and Julie, ranging in years from thirteen down to ten or so. They haven't seen their dad in a month, and they clamber over him like one of his stories. Tom seems a decade younger.

Hey, listen to this.

Weird. I suggested a short story to an editor of a hi-fi magazine on an audio nut. He bought the idea. I wrote the story. A weird story about an audio nut who becomes his equipment. The editor loved the story and he's doing it. Should be out in a few months in *Modern Hi-Fi & Stereo Guide.* How about that! Fiction is breaking out all over.

—10/21/76

Jarrel held the stick of dynamite in his hand. He could feel the power in his hands, like it was something alive, something that would live for only the briefest time. He watched the wick sputter and fizzle, coming closer to the stick. He was fascinated with it. So much force in such a small stick. Soon it was going to explode, to shatter, to blow apart everything in its path. There was nothing that could stand up to it. It would reduce everything to the same democratic rubble. He wanted to be there when it blew up and he was tempted to hold it in his hands when it went off, perhaps knowing for the briefest fraction of a second what all that power was like before it tore his head off and then blew him apart into liquid bits, spraying pieces of him along with everything else in one gigantic mist of power (*Temporary Sanity,* p. 11).

The Glynn family in transit are like a band of gypsies on a run of bad luck. Pat and the kids have been autoing through the West while Tom winds up an issue of *Neighborhood* (he's become managing editor for the New York Urban Coalition, a group dedicated to revitalizing run-down parts of the city).

The kids are crabby from the travelling, Pat is weary from the kids, and Tom has been spoiled by a month of peace. They're all set to take off for Michigan when their veteran Saab (I love New York! its rear bumper says, and it looks it) develops a bad list to starboard.

"Alignment?" Tom asks the mechanic.

"Cracked A-frame," the mechanic replies. "One week."

You won't believe what I've been writing, Jerry. I mean while you and Jon and everybody else is writing important things, critiques, fictions, and the like, I am writing articles on CB antennas for electronic magazines, I am writing articles on successful hi-fi dealers, I am writing capsule descriptions of eighty of the most important companies in the CB market. How's that for your old artistic principles????? A jab up the ass of fiction? A quaff down the old throat of Kulture?????

The only time I get to write fiction is when I do some freelance advertising copy.

—7/19/76

Glynn finds poetry in the special nature of the Adirondacks: the devastated economics, the dirt poor people whose very minds are oddly deprived (the book's action's concerns Jarrel and Jeeter trying to blow their brother Lester out of the state asylum), and especially how the seasons lock in on this beautiful but vulnerable land.

Because the book's language makes us share thought and spirit with the brothers, we understand their pleasures— rather, Glynn's writing sings the joy of their enthusiasms. Running the county blacktops in a stolen ¾-ton pickup— four wheel drive, hi-beams and all. Or just the thought of snow crushing down the barn roof: snow, melting to ice, then more snow, and more.

Temporary Sanity is about a deeper realism, the imaginative life we wouldn't otherwise know was there.

Tom and Pat, and their kids. Clarence, with Jonathan Baumbach, who has brought along son Noah for the ride. The Brooklyn kids take on the Iowa kids at basketball, and guess who wins? Huge pots of ribs, rolling out noodles for tomorrow's casserole at 2:00 A.M., two days of solid rain and bitchiness on the screen porch. Siobahn is a strict vegetarian and a bit ill for it. Brendan plays all the Eric Clapton records, still wants Bruce Springsteen when his folks want to go to bed. Nobody is talking about fiction. Tom helps fix the hi-fi.

The farms were small clearings sunk deep in the forest. Some bordered on each other, others, hateful at the thought of another human face, were stuck way out by themselves, often at the end of rutted trails that were almost unpassable in winter. Everything seemed to shrink in size on these farms. The barns were smaller, the houses tiny, even the cows and goats and chickens seemed miniature versions of those in the lowlands. The houses were built of plywood and sheetrock and corrugated iron. Sheets of plastic were tacked up at the windows. Nothing seemed to be whole. A screen door had a hinge broke. Tape was stuck over a broken window. Roofing shingles were used in place of warped slats of wood that came off the sides (*Temporary Sanity*, pp. 35–36).

Don't blink your eyes going through DeKalb; otherwise you'll miss the whole town. You'll pass a general store-gas station on the right, then the road curves to the left. Before the road straightens out again, there is a bridge to the left (this is about 100 or so yards from the general store). Go over the bridge. Continue on that road for a mile or so, you'll pass a dairy farm, go up a hill, and then take the first road to the right. This is the road we are on. Go down that road and we are the third barn (or fourth if you count the empty barn at the turnoff) on the left—if in doubt check the mailbox opposite, it will say GLYNN, Box 45A (not 45), and that's us.

—8/1/76

From Grand Central, take the IRT express to Brooklyn. Get off at Nevins Avenue in Brooklyn. Walk across platform and take Seventh Avenue IRT. Then get off at Grand Army Plaza (third stop). Subway exit is opposite newsstand, walk opposite way on Flatbush Avenue to Sterling Place. Turn left, we are two blocks.

—6/1/77

You can take the D train to Brooklyn and get off at Seventh Avenue, climb the northeast stairs to the street, duck under the exhaust fan that fills the subway entrance with the smells of barbeque chicken and ribs, stroll past the Haitian barbershop jammed with checker players, then amble down Carlton Avenue and see brownstones with elegant windows and beautifully molded ceilings in between decayed rooming houses and cinderblocked-up buildings.

—"Where is Prospect Heights?", *Neighborhood,* 6/78

"Bo and Be," from *Statements 2* (Fiction Collective, 1977) is a sample of Tom Glynn's urban fiction. But it is remarkably like his upstate stuff. Here we have two city hillbillies, "senior citizens," old and fat and deformed and mentally short. The subway is an adventure of muggers and insults. Their very lives are absurd, as in a Beckett play. The story comes through their perception, and Glynn explains his method. He likes to deal with people whose information-gathering ability is somewhat askew. Perception, epistemology, the dancing language of life: these are Tom Glynn's angels.

The Glynns are gone! The Saab is fixed, they've rented a Mercury Monarch on our Visa card in the meantime, Jon and Clarence are in New York by now in Jon's more dependable rented Buick, and it is all quiet and peaceful again. For a long weekend, Iowa was a corner of Brooklyn, a noisy and crazy quarter with writers and kids coming out the doors, out the windows.

After five weeks of cooking out of the back seat, Pat has given up and left us the foodstuffs and paraphernalia. Six months later, her box of Handi-Wrap is still going strong.

Criterion for the new fiction: Not reality or unreality, or coming to grips with some great moral problem, or lack of same, but something else. For want of a better word, I call it energy. Thomas's "the force that through this green fuse drives, . . ." I know I misquoted it, but that's the idea. Not the words, nor the great writing, not the plot, not the situation, not the avant-gardism nor rear-gardism, but the energy, the force of a work that pushes through like some great tornado orgasm. That is what to look for. That is what I am trying to do.

—10/21/74

Subtext: The Critic *par lui-même*

Innovative Fiction (1972)

As Ishmael Reed notes in passing within his *God Made Alaska for the Indians* (New York: Garland Press, 1982), there is "Hughes Rudd, whose appearance in experimental anthologies alongside Barthelme and Barth is a well-kept secret" (p. 52). What's important is not just that he's an innovative fictionist, but that for thirty years he's responded to the behavior of mainstream America on its favorite medium, Nielsen-ranked #1 CBS network TV. If this isn't accessibility, what is? For any revolution, aesthetic or otherwise, cannot be successful until it has been assimilated into the middle class. Hughes Rudd, telling metafictional stories each early morning on the CBS News, reaches the middle class and stays there by his success within it.

Innovative Fiction uses the same strategy of middle-class acceptability: a ranking of stories from familiar to exotic, from easy to difficult, beginning with Kurt Vonnegut whose "The Hyannis Port Story" used this same structure to ease its in-

tended *Saturday Evening Post* readers into the wild brinksmanship of the Kennedy/go-go years. "The farthest away from
home I ever sold a storm window," his narrator begins, "was
in Hyannis Port, Massachusetts, practically in the front yard
of President Kennedy's summer home." He measures all distances from his own hometown of North Crawford, New
Hampshire—as good a center to the universe as anyone
might contrive. Entering Hyannis, he plots a careful course
from the predictability of the Presidential Motor Inn and the
First Family Waffle Shop to the marginal fringe of the PT-109
Cocktail Lounge and a miniature golf course called "The
New Frontier." Encountering fame, he shucks off Adlai Ste-
venson with some neighborly back-fence talk and maintains
workmanlike diffidence as he installs his storms and screens
amid Hyannis's riches and Kennedy-Goldwater animosities.
There are cultural innovations galore, but without this middle-class evaluation they might as well be meaningless scrib-
bles. Vonnegut's tradesman is a reader in the text, and without him nothing is legible.

That the 1960s were American fiction's decade of innovation is obvious from this simplicity-to-complexity structure.
In any previous decade, the avant-garde is just that, so isolated in its advance position that there are few points of relation
to the general culture. *Outré* is the name of the game, from
Henry Miller in Paris to the Beats in San Francisco. But in
the American 1960s, one can start with Vonnegut, who's
been around for a decade in the *Saturday Evening Post* and now
leads the bestseller list with *Slaughterhouse-Five,* and from there
take a small step to Hughes Rudd's comic posturings and
Richard Brautigan's self-dramatizing metaphors. Even Ber-
nard Malamud, as comfortable as a pair of old slippers, can
slip in some innovative magic with a talking bird, this one
small change making all his usual conventions seem radically

different. Then Amiri Baraka's self-created world of language (yet recognizable as the flurry of a college dorm), Robert Coover's spatial restructuring of time (yet familiar as
channel switching on TV), and Donald Barthelme's recy-
cling of our culture's junk into strange new sculptures of
words and attitudes. A dozen and a half small steps take us
from Vonnegut to the syntactic energy of Ron Sukenick's
"Momentum," as innovative as any avant-garde explosion
but, in the 1960s context, as accessible as any of the deliberate steps in between. "i had hold of myself had hold of my experience no had hold of a level of experience   that i mustn't
ever lose sight of again," his story concludes, having taken
the reader through the visceral experience of flying through
his nonstop sentences as he struggles to record them. The
decade's creative energy has been shared in Sukenick's textual momentum. The common readers are never spurned or
even accidentally left out. Instead, the story's structure has
seized them by their necks and ankles and swept them into its
dance of life. This story, this anthology, and this decade in
general have taken readers into fiction's text and shot them
out of it like a cannon ball. As John Barth's concluding
"Autobiography" explains, "I'll mutter to the end, one word
after another, string the rascals out, mad or not, heard or not,
my last words will be my last words."

The Vonnegut Statement (1973)

Another book coedited with John Somer, but this time
with original essays by various hands. "The chapters which
follow were completed with an eye to each other; indeed, they
may be among the first essays in criticism written in part and
revised by long-distance telephone." Reviewers agree that it

works, the *New York Review of Books* calling it "the first signs of a new sociology of academe." Scholarship is out of the library and into parties, picnics, keggers, love affairs, brawls, and reunions—social points of the times where the book's twelve contributors assemble like apostles to complete their evangelical work.

This too is another sign of the times: after working in obscurity for nearly twenty years and struggling for the right form for his necessary message, Vonnegut has broken through with *Slaughterhouse-Five* and is now embraced as the age's guru. His critics are enthusiasts, testifying not simply to Vonnegut's literary art but to his power to change lives. Rather than fight this tendency, *The Vonnegut Statement* embraces it and takes it for its own method. We are determined to be honest about our excitement and not disguise it with drapes of pedantry. Remember those English profs from Columbia and Rutgers who wrote the first jazz criticism two generations ago? At 5:00 P.M. they'd knock off from a day's work scanning lines of poetry and embrace swing and bebop jazz with all the modishness of eighteenth-century gentleman slumming it down Gin Lane. The resulting criticism was wooden and forced, seeking as it did the formal perfection of a sonnet or villanelle in every trumpet solo. Vonnegut deserved better than this.

And so a book of essays on his literary history (years of toil followed by epic success), formal craft (narrative structure in *Mother Night,* language of the inanimate in *Player Piano,* apocalyptic vision in *Slaughterhouse-Five*), and cultural impact (teaching KV to the earth-shoes & granola set, or rather them teaching KV to us). But for all the footnotes which managed to sneak in, *The Vonnegut Statement* is more about its makers than its subject. And what a treat for us, since it was reviewed in *Time* magazine, right in their love-power/rock-and-roll issue with Janis Joplin on the cover. Vonnegut was taken seriously, and so were we. This was a big first step toward devising a new criticism to accompany *Innovative Fiction*'s texts.

Kurt Vonnegut, Jr.: A Descriptive Bibliography and Annotated Secondary Checklist (1974)

   Enthusiasm, yes. But facile impressionism, definitely no. Therefore the need to be as responsible to the contemporary as one must be to any previous literary epoch. So off to the library, not to reaffirm an older critical method but rather to see what descriptive bibliography might reveal about our new subject. Confirmation that the early Vonnegut did in fact publish in obscurity: only 7,600 copies of his first novel, *Player Piano,* in 1952, for example, with less than half being sold—"and most of those in Schenectady, New York," the author admitted, where he'd lived for three years and found a model for his work. Even less for Vonnegut's next three hardcovers—2,500 copies, 5,500, and 6,000. Only with *God Bless You, Mr. Rosewater* in 1965 does he see a second printing, and then only a modest edition of 6,000 copies following the first run of 7,000, and this during the year in which his short story market among the family magazines had dried up completely. From 1950 on, when he'd quit his publicist's job with General Electric and moved to Cape Cod, Vonnegut had published five stories per year (at $750 to $2,000 per story) in such middle-brow journals as *Collier's* and the *Saturday Evening Post,* but by the mid-1960s they were out of business and Vonnegut was up against a financial wall. His "The Hyannis Port Story," of which we made so much for *Innovative Fiction,* tells a tale even for bibliographers: written with the *Post* in mind and accepted for a late November issue, it had to be cancelled in galleys because of President Kennedy's assassination. With all this data in hand, there was no need to be simply evangelical about Vonnegut's struggles in obscurity, for hard evidence supported the argument at every turn.

Yet even obscurity has features to reveal under the inquiring light. Writing stories for *Collier's* and the *Post* would put Vonnegut near the heart of his popular culture, but consider the constellation of popular figures which resulted when he helped adapt one of his texts, "D. P.," for presentation on television's "General Electric Theatre." The host, of course, was Ronald Reagan, and the playlet was used to introduce Sammy Davis, Jr., in his first dramatic role—on October 5, 1958, as the critic started high school. Even for the contemporary period, archaeology can be needed.

The research for Vonnegut's bibliography turn up so many uncollected stories, and especially such a wide range of essays and reviews produced by Vonnegut in the middle and later 1960s when his story markets had disappeared, that an anthology of these works could be presented to his publishers at Dell. *Rare Vonnegut,* we called it. "That sounds utterly posthumous," Vonnegut complained, but let the essays be published nevertheless. The coincidence of a master writer having to turn to book reviews and commentary just as the popular culture was exploding is another happy accident bibliography can uncover; Vonnegut's pieces on the Maharishi, the Apollo moon shots, Biafra, and the arms race are not only good writing but are indices to his literary method, more apparent here because its subject is something real life shares. In his Preface, Vonnegut thanked us and called us archaeologists, recognizing the impulse behind our bibliography. Dell paid us $500 for our work, a flat fee for *Wampeters, Foma &*

Granfalloons: Opinions, which quickly ran through several hardcover and quality paperback printings and scores of rack-size issues. It is Vonnegut's best selling book after his novels.

Literary Disruptions (1975)

"The making of a post-contemporary American fiction," reads its subtitle, and in that taunt is the first point of its polemics. Scholarship and even literate readership lacks a sense of currency: Norman Mailer, over fifty years old at the time, is described by critics as a "young writer," a man "at the leading edge" of fictive innovation. "New" writers such as John Updike and Philip Roth are scarcely ten years younger, while the issue of serious innovation is sidetracked by featuring John Barth and Thomas Pynchon, whose experimental complexities keep them safely inert. In terms of literary history, it is almost as if Vonnegut hasn't happened.

And so the solid base of his innovations, as projected stylistically by *Innovative Fiction* and *The Vonnegut Statement* and supported by the data of the *Bibliography,* is used to launch *Literary Disruptions.* "Fiction breeds its own continuity," and looking back to other benchmarks in literary history—Hawthorne and Melville in 1851, Howells-Twain-James in 1885, and Hemingway and Fitzgerald in 1925—the innovations by Vonnegut & Company which occupy the late 1960s show more of a pattern. From here, take another series of small steps forward, as did the texts of *Innovative Fiction,* and you'll find Vonnegut marvelling at how his younger colleague Donald Barthelme can use the pages of the *New Yorker* magazine to educate a readership to the new fiction (just as composers must find musicians who can play these new works), and their mutual friend Jerzy Kosinski paralleling their formal innovations with similar developments in theme.

Vonnegut begins with a vision, born of the Dresden massacre which he witnessed as a prisoner of war and which existing forms simply can't accommodate. His first five novels, from *Player Piano* through *Rosewater,* are attempts to find a shape for this apocalyptic insight, and while successful in their own ways these fictions stop short of articulating the ineffable. "What do you say about a massacre?" Vonnegut asks himself in the first chapter of *Slaughterhouse-Five* (1969) and in this reflexive honesty finds a way to confront his novel's formal challenge. The real subject of this book is his writing of it, and so its opening and concluding chapters (most definitely not a conventional preface and afterword) show him at work, struggling to get it underway and then anguishing at its result. This strategy of putting himself within his work as its self-apparent creator had been tried in 1963 with the manuscript of *Cat's Cradle,* only to be rejected by his publishers. In 1966, for the hardcover re-edition of *Mother Night,* Vonnegut added a clarifying introduction which described his own involvement in the "monkey business" of World War II, and for his stories collected in 1968 as *Welcome to the Monkey House* he again spent several pages talking about himself and his personal approach to literary methods. The death of Kurt Vonnegut's short story markets, for which he'd written stories with foolproof formulas intuited from his own reading of American culture and made explicit in his anthropology thesis from the University of Chicago, "Fluctuations between Good and Evil in Simple Tales," had kept his attention focused on literary craft. Once he began writing commentary for *Esquire,* the *New York Times Magazine,* and other journals, the evolving form of New Journalism—which placed the reporter at the center of events from which he could comment most directly on himself—provided Vonnegut with hands-on experience treating his act of authorship as a prime ingredient in the work before him.

With Donald Barthelme, language itself takes center stage, a logical progression from Vonnegut's fascination with authorship toward the objectivization of its product. So often in postmodern culture, words do a poor job of matching up with the reality they supposedly describe. Consider the argot of advertising, in which *authentic* means *a reproduction,* as in "an authentic reproduction of Early American." *Fresh* can signify *frozen,* as with "fresh-frozen orange juice." And so forth. In Barthelme's hands, such language no longer attempts to do such off-center signifying work, but rather becomes an object itself, admirable for its artifice and not its signification. "Signs are signs," one of his beleaguered characters admits, "and some of them are lies." But in making that admission, a more satisfactory verbal art becomes possible, based on the truth that people communicate not through essences of meaning but by linguistic fabrications which can be of great interest in themselves.

What Vonnegut and Barthelme accomplish on formal grounds, Jerzy Kosinski achieves with the thematic. Of all contemporary American writers, he has the most apparent "story" to tell—of being orphaned in the war, terrorized by brutal peasants, then reunited with his family only to face the oppressions of postwar collectivization. As a young man, he flees Poland for the West, finding in America not only a social system in which to live freely but a language which allows him to express himself in fiction. But this story demands a disruption of conventional thematics, for the self his protagonists liberate can be a fearsome monster as well. Traumatized in the languages of his childhood, Polish and Russian,

Kosinski finds that he cannot write freely in them today. But English, learned abstractly as an adult, responds to his command and allows him to express himself (and not some predetermined social behavior). So language is part of this author's scheme of innovations. But central to his work is Kosinski's belief that the self, whose alienation was so routinely lamented among the modernists, is something whose power has not been properly reckoned with. To unleash it calls for more consideration than had been taken heretofore.

The childhood experience in Poland throws Kosinski's story into high relief, but its American compatibility is shown by the similar thematics of James Park Sloan, a white southerner from a family of military careerists, and Imamu Amiri Baraka, a northern black city dweller (whose name had been LeRoi Jones in the earlier part of his career). But the strongest American innovations are found in the works of Raymond Federman, Gilbert Sorrentino, and Ronald Sukenick. Like Kosinski, Federman is an immigrant with a war orphan's experience. Less fortunate than his Polish colleague, Federman had lost his parents and sisters to the camps but escaped like his future mentor Samuel Beckett to work on agricultural communes in the south of France. His writing strategy, however, is the opposite of Kosinski's: he will avoid the need for simply thematic innovation by means of a formal stroke, *not writing* about his orphan's experience at all. Instead, the deaths of his parents and two sisters are indicated by the figures XXXX, a concrete design within the typography of his books, all of which depend upon the visual impression of typing on the page. His first novel, *Double or Nothing,* is itself a procrastination at writing: the epic record of a novelist plotting out all the essentials he'll need to lock himself up for a year to write his great story, right down to calculating how many boxes of noodles, squeezes of toothpaste, and sheets of toilet tissue he'll need to survive. These computations take all 200 pages of his oversized publication, itself the photographed typescript pages each of which has a unique spatial design reminding us that its materiality alone is the story's substance. The text's multidimensionality comes via its authors: the first person who records, the second person who invents what the first person records, the third person whose experiences are invented, and a fourth person (suggested by Federman's colleague at Buffalo, John Barth) to supervise the workings of the three and produce the book at hand.

As one might guess, none of the four ever gets his work done, for at the last moment the computation of supplies is found to be in error, and the whole process must start again—guaranteeing the life of fiction! With Federman, thankfully, nothing ever ends. In *Take It or Leave It,* his protagonist sets out to cross America but never gets farther than upstate New York; but this is sufficient to fill an entire novel, as his misadventures, wrong turns, and obstructions create a better fiction than he'd imagined when plotting out his future life. As we'll see in *The Self-Apparent Word* nearly a decade later, Federman will develop this technique into the essence of narrative itself.

Sorrentino's contribution is a comic self-consciousness of novel writing's business: sarcastically footnoting expressions he dislikes, rigging the action to embarrass characters he hates, and rearranging everything to remind us that art is something different from and often much richer than life. Without the awkward mechanics of self-reflexion, he manages to suspend the suspension of disbelief, replacing linear continuity with the spatial juxtaposition of reality—reflecting not reality itself but rather its processes. This generational sense of composition is pushed to its fullest in the work of

Ronald Sukenick, who revalidates our imaginations so that we can look at experience in a new way. For him, fiction is not about experience, it is more experience—at its best, simply a perfection of living, and liable to go afoul only when preconceptions of form step in. Like a sorcerer, Sukenick stops the world, calling a halt to having a culture's provisional view of reality accepted as absolute, and allows the imagination to reinvent according to its needs. This is how we stay in touch.

One of the first sentences Ronald Sukenick published, at the start of his Brandeis dissertation soon published as *Wallace Stevens: Musing the Obscure* (New York: New York University Press, 1967), sums up his aesthetic and the thesis behind *Literary Disruptions* as well: "When, through the imagination, the ego manages to reconcile reality with its own needs, the formerly insipid landscape is infused with the ego's emotion; and reality, since it now seems intensely relevant to the ego, suddenly seems more real" (pp. 14–15).

The Life of Fiction (1977)

Literary Disruption's method had been directly historical, the record of a decade's innovations with attention given to roots, mutual influence, and development—a conventional work of scholarship. But what of the critical energies, bred of a life within the new fiction, which had been necessarily left out? The aesthetics of Sukenick and his colleagues had overturned the Aristotelian assumptions on which conventional fiction had been based; might the methods of literary criticism be changed as well?

As with the fiction of Sukenick and Federman, the energy of *Literary Disruptions* had been in the writing of it, and that writing had been an especially active pursuit: travelling around the country to meet these writers, to party and drink with them, taping interviews in bars and apartments and once over the clatter of tools in a roommate-sculptor's studio; phone calls here and there; writers' visits to Cedar Falls with readings, receptions, parties, assignations, and 5:00 A.M. breakfasts after nonstop nights; scraps of bibliography, snippits of reviews and essays and whatnot these fictionists had written with their left hands but which now reveal a literary method.

Scattered across the desktop, these bits and pieces form a spatial collage, the materials of a new criticism at work among themselves, making statements by juxtaposition and by the very fact of having been collected and assembled. And so for *The Life of Fiction:* photograph the desktop. Roy Behrens is called in to help with the design. *The Vonnegut Statement* was created by long-distance telephone, and its structure reflected this communal act. But *The Life of Fiction*'s method is participatory with the text itself, text here being not just the writing but the entire context which produces it. Indeed, for Sukenick and his colleagues in style, there is no distinction between living and writing, and so for the criticism there is no distinction between its process and the final product. In both cases, it's a question of energy which must be captured on the page, and a sense of spatial juxtaposition which the reader himself or herself creates does the job.

Much of this book recapitulates *Literary Disruptions* in terms of judgment: Sorrentino, Sukenick, Barthelme, and Vonnegut are all here. But Hunter S. Thompson broadens the coverage, taking in the creative energy (a true life of fiction) exploited by personal journalism. And with full chapters on Steve Katz, Ishmael Reed, Clarence Major, Jonathan Baumbach, and Russell Banks, the innovative edge is that much sharper. But the volume's key feature is that of *life:* a kinetic life on the page when read, expressing the organic process of the critical act forming itself and taking place. No wonder the critic is caught up into the lives of some new subjects here, notably Walter Abish and Michael Stephens. Sipping espresso in Walter's garden, roaming Broadway south of Columbia with Michael on the night of Nixon's resignation. Heading back to Michael's sub-let on West 110th Street and listening to a tape of his reading a few weeks before—the passage from *Season at Coole* with Mother Rose drunk on Vodka in her laundry room, "dreamless, alone, phantom-like in motherhood, a little Catholic school girl playing hooky from her holy family."

Donald Barthelme: A Comprehensive Bibliography (1977)

For a writer whom fame and age have taken out of touch, more sorting through the shards of archaeology. The research is not meant to document an epic struggle such as Vonnegut's, but what we do find is that this seemingly abstract writer has been just as deeply immersed within the popular culture. For all his Philadelphia-born and *New Yorker*–published sophistication, there's an east Texas twang to Barthelme's writing voice which will emerge with the confidence of his later works. And here are the roots: high school juvenilia about the full-blown romance of "Miss Amanda Feverish, Southern belle," a parody of *Pilgrim's Progress* as "Rover Boys' Retrogression." Then daily reviews for the Houston *Post* of movies, circuses, and night club acts. Abbott and Costello at the Orpheum, Greer Garson at Loew's; "Singing Newsman Bing Crosby in Pursuit of Jane Wyman" reads one headline. The 466-item list of his writings before *New Yorker* days reads like a concordance to his stories.

Vonnegut in America (1977)

Another collaborative anthology, this time more staid as most of it comes from an MLA super-session on Vonnegut. But the title piece, "Vonnegut in America," outlines a thesis in historical development. Examine Kurt's biography and you'll find clear roots for his themes and innovative styles: the notion of uncritical love from his happy life among a large, extended family in the American Midwest; a lesson on how arbitrary reality can be when he sees his family lose its fortune in the Great Depression; another chance at the artifice of extended families when he discovers frat life at Cornell (where he also studies science); the rude awakening to what science can accomplish at the firebombing of Dresden; more cultural relativism, including the notion that everything, even our most deeply held notions of absolutes, are all invented, as he studies anthropology in graduate school at Chicago; another view of research scientists as innocently bumbling fools next door as he works as their publicist at General Electric's Research Lab ("Progress Is Our Most Important Product"). Then a brave plunge into the world of full-time fiction writing, yet not as an isolated artist *manqué* but rather among the businessmen and tradesmen of West Barnstable, Massachusetts, where for twenty years he operates a cottage industry manufacturing short stories for *Collier's* and the *Post* which memorialize the same class he lives within. From these life-events come his innovative novels, but this same biography—midwestern family life, college, military service, grad school on the G. I. Bill, white-collar work for a big postwar corporation, and finally his own small business—fits that of the typical male from Vonnegut's generation. Perhaps this is why his fictions have become so popular, so accessible to a public which shuns the avant-garde. How can Vonnegut have succeeded both as an innovative novelist and as a cozily familiar writer for family magazines? Here may be an answer.

Writing Under Fire: Stories of the Vietnam War (1978)

Another literary cultural parallel: America enters the 1960s with its art forms stable and its international presence secure, and ends the decade with both blown out of recognition. More parallels: each movement, aesthetic and political, shares an anti-authoritarian structure, abandons linear continuity for spatial form, and celebrates the imaginative by defying the real. "Unreal" is the era's catchword. But here's the closest parallel of all: the Vietnam war rejects previous stereotypes; it can not be described with either traditional historical or fictional forms, and so a new way of writing about it has to be invented. Michael Herr's *Dispatches* creates the same innovations for reporting Vietnam which Vonnegut, Brautigan, and Sukenick have been perfecting for fiction at home. The American 1960s have been a special decade, so more on this later.

The Diaries of Willard Motley (1979)

An editorial project which uncovers a new style of realism: not documentary but lyrical, not sociological in purpose but rather phenomenological. And another life of fiction: as an experimental naturalist in prose, Motley saved everything—to be discovered moldering in his niece's basement on Chicago's South Side and crying for critical arrangement. Arrangement as interpretation, *The Life of Fiction* again. So close once more to the act of writing. On one side of his desk Motley keeps his diary, on the other his manuscript of *Knock On Any Door.* Sometimes the two cannot be distinguished. "Tuesday June 1st, 1943: Nick died at 8 o'clock tonight. So, the book is finished and now, with typing, I can send it out. I'm not as happy about ending as I felt I would be. I hadn't realized how long three and a half years are nor how dear Nick had grown to me. I feel as if one of my arms had been cut off. Three and a half years of my life—ten years of Nick's life. Killing him hurt a lot—I ended with tears in my eyes." Motley mentions trying to start on his new book right away but gets only into a couple pages. "Then, thinking about Nick, went out for a few beers. Met Morry. Had a few more—and a couple shots of whiskey. Got drunk." A good place to end.

The Practice of Fiction in America (1980)

"In a sense, all American fiction is experimental"—Hawthorne struggling against the natural gloom of his materials for an ill-advised happy ending, Howells anguishing over the contrary claims of ethic and aesthetic, Kate Chopin perfecting literary naturalism in a play of image and symbol, F. Scott Fitzgerald developing from saturation to selection, Faulkner finding both theme and technique in the notion of community, Motley awash in phenomenological realism, Updike cultivating and then reharvesting himself, Vonnegut's self-dramatization as real-life reflexivity, and Donald Barthelme's art of collage. "Avant-garde and After" brings us to today, just ten small steps back to Hawthorne.

The American 1960s (1980)

Pretend John F. Kennedy and Richard Nixon are fiction writers, and *Profiles in Courage* and *Six Crises* their novels. The images, styles of characterization, and structural symbology become apt portals for the decade, which opens with Kennedy's lofty promise and ends with Nixon's closely played, less than imaginative attempt to manage it all. From wild brinksmanship to an end of adventure. Yet for all its concluding conservativism, the 1960s have suffered only a half step back from its giant strides forward, and a new reality has been created within which Americans will live, by standards undreamt of twenty years before.

Now think of Ken Kesey's McMurphy and Joseph Heller's Yossarian as politicians, the former blasting open the confines of a mental ward with his consciousness-raising self-assertion, the latter stripping international politics of its wacky, ungeared teeth. *One Flew Over the Cuckoo's Nest* and *Catch-22,* two more gateways to the 1960s, novels which project a good picture of its developing ethics and aesthetics. Later in the decade, Vonnegut and Barthelme will clarify its image in a self-conscious play of signs, while James Kunen and Hunter S. Thompson make of its journalism a song of oneself. In music it comes out as Bob Dylan and Neil Young, in painting as the revolution within and against Abstract Expressionism which granted the artist the possibilities of innovation within a supposedly exhausted conceptual world. The artistic act becomes itself, since all that's left is an encounter with materials. But Harold Rosenberg's dictum from the 1950s, that the canvas now becomes less of a surface upon which to represent than an arena within which to act, is now playable by the entire culture. The museums are closed, for this is the age of Performance.

Literary Disruptions, Second Edition (1980)

As the writers studied half a decade ago have developed their careers, writing two or three new books each, they've become increasingly self-critical about the innovative issues they have raised. The literary climate has encouraged this, characterized as it's been not just by works like *Literary Disruptions,* Bob Scholes's *The Fabulators,* and Tony Tanner's *City of Words,* but also by the skepticism of Gardner's *On Moral Fiction* and Graff's *Literature Against Itself.* Hence, Vonnegut refines his autobiographical intrusion into a structural method for *Breakfast of Champions* and as an imaginative fantasy in *Slapstick,* while Kosinski pushes his protagonists even farther into manic solipsism even as he approaches in *Blind Date* the previously unutterable material of the Tate-Polanski murders—killings of his closest friends, on an evening he himself was supposed to be there.

The greatest refinements are technical: Barthelme reducing his stories to the barest lines of dialogue which without benefit or need of context can be sallied back and forth as almost pure language; Sukenick developing through his *Disgressions* essays a coherent literary theory which elucidates his compositionally energistic fiction in *Long Talking Bad Conditions Blues;* and Gilbert Sorrentino exhausting the techniques of exhaustion itself with *Mulligan Stew,* in which every innovation of the 1960s is effectively written into the ground. All to clear the ground for the more open fields of self-apparency and experimental realism.

Kurt Vonnegut (1982)

Building upon the earlier theses about his storehouse of popular culture and development of literary vision from the biographical bench marks of his life, this is a study of form, of the intertextuality imbedded within the stages of Vonnegut's career. First, the get-even, tell-it-all novel anyone can write— *Player Piano*—which for its structure borrows the dystopian

form familiar from George Orwell's success of a few years before, *1984*. Then science fiction for *The Sirens of Titan,* the spy
novel for *Mother Night,* apocalypse for *Cat's Cradle,* and a
prince-and-the-pauper form for *God Bless You, Mr. Rosewater*—
popular subgenres all. Experiment works its way into the
process as early as *Mother Night,* with ever-increasing doses of
autobiography and self-reflexion. At first it's thematic, then
with *Slaughterhouse-Five* becomes a matter of technique in that
the opening and closing chapters frame the tale. *Breakfast of
Champions* puts Vonnegut inside his novel's actions and its
techniques, making it his first fully "personal novel," a mode
in which he continues through today.

Peter Handke and the Postmodern Transformation (1983)

With James Knowlton, who handles the works not yet
translated into English. But Handke is a thoroughly international writer, having returned to Austria only after living in
Paris for a decade. His English is perfect, and his familiarity
with American culture, both pop and traditional, informs
many of his novels. In many respects, he is the emblematic
postmodern man.

Short Letter, Long Farewell is set in the United States, a country Handke finds to be a semiotic self-apparency where signs
refer to themselves as naturally as to what they are presumed
to represent—in this way the postmodern novel, as a play of
signs rather than of events, becomes a thoroughly accessible
work. America is a land of surfaces; what you see is what
there is. In Europe, Handke's protagonists founder amid the
linguistic confusion explained so well by Wittgenstein: every
problem is essentially a problem in language, since the signs
we are forced to deal with are not identical with reality, that

out-of-reach chimera which vexes our every act. But the U.S. boasts a special *significant* nature, having sprung fully formed from the minds of its creators and sustained by a tradition of symbolism. Even in politics, with the House Un-American Activities Committee? Only in America, we must admit; for what in England could be un-British activities? Or across the channel, un-French?

In the cross-country tradition of Nabokov's *Lolita,* Handke travels from coast to coast and border to border across this land of self-apparent surfaces. Seeing everything as a sign for itself, from gaudy motels to historic emblems of the pioneers which idealize the country's history in each day's drive, celebrating the land's self-conscious identity at every mundane occasion: this is the imaginative reinvention of reality, much as America itself began as "the New World" that Handke's narrator encounters at every turn and that he sees expressed so well in our literature.

In all his works, Handke shows protagonists encountering worlds of signs rather than the world itself. In some cases, the circumstance is pathological, as when in *The Goalie's Anxiety at the Penalty Kick* his hero suspends the semiotic process and so isolates himself from existence. But against the fears of the moral fiction critics, Handke shows how novels written within the postmodern axioms of a signifier and signified need not be icily inhuman, abstract affairs. Literature is a way of looking at the world, both sides of this debate agree. Glancing out his window one day, Handke noticed two foreign workers sweeping the street beneath his apartment. Both were wearing orange and white striped jackets *like bicycle racers,* he observed; baggy pants *like bums* or *characters in a Beckett play,* hats *like POWs,* and so forth—faces *like Southern Europeans,* stiff knees and flat feet *like drunks,* armed with gigantic brooms and shovels *like figures in a painting by Breughel.* Soon Handke had to admit that he was seeing not the guestworkers, but rather the terms of relationship between them and other things. No real object was present to him, only a system of differences. Casting out his net to capture reality, Handke had drawn back with his object unsnared. And yet something very strange had happened: once this process took over as an automatic activity, as it does so naturally in our day-to-day lives, reality became the net itself.

The Self-Apparent Word (1984)

Fiction as language, language as fiction. All as a way of facing the ultimate challenge to fiction as an art form. In all the other arts, postmodern theory had worked successfully to remove representation and replace it with the materiality of the work itself. No problem in painting or music, for daubs of paint and notes of sound need not refer to something else: they can be most naturally themselves. But for writing, there's the problem that its most fundamental component, language, points to a meaning beyond the page: words cannot simply be themselves, as they refer to a reality for which they are the commonly accepted signpost. Nonsense, cut-ups, and graphic collages only frustrate this process, replacing it with nothing positive in itself.

But realizing that these references to the outside world are only a system of differences, one can then embrace the system itself as an object, as its own reality. As the deconstructionists would say, the signifiers (words and phrases) need no longer be considered as transparent windows to another reality (the signified), but can be embraced in their opacity as real substances by themselves. Pulling down the blinds on the outside world hence lets us see our own activity more clearly. Man is the sign-making animal, and placing the business of fiction on this level does not remove it from the human sphere but makes it more naturally human than the Aristotelian, imitative form which went before.

With this in mind, true fiction again becomes possible. Even the conventions of realism can be recovered for self-apparent use as signs. Within this dispensation, there is even a role for the critic. Were he a Frenchman, he might cite Roland Barthes and claim "It must all be considered as if spoken by a character in a novel." But far better to think of Kurt Vonnegut, that fellow middle-class midwesterner of his own father's generation, style, and temperament, who when prefacing his collected stories thought back to a review which called his work "a series of narcissistic giggles." "Perhaps it would be helpful to the reader to imagine me as the White Rock girl," Vonnegut suggests, "kneeling on a boulder in a nightgown, either looking for minnows or adoring her own reflection."

Index